£6.95

The Refugee Crisis

ISSUES

Volume 5

Editor

Craig Donnellan

Independence

Educational Publishers
Cambridge

First published by Independence
PO Box 295
Cambridge CB1 3XP
England

© Craig Donnellan 2002

British Library Cataloguing in Publication Data
The Refugee Crisis – (Issues Series)
I. Donnellan, Craig II. Series
362.8'7

ISBN 1 86168 202 6

Printed in Great Britain
The Burlington Press
Cambridge

Typeset by
Claire Boyd

Cover
The illustration on the front cover is by
Pumpkin House.

CONTENTS

Overview

Chapter One: Refugees and Asylum Seekers

0006681099 0010

Introduction

The Refugee Crisis is the fifth volume in the **Issues** series. The aim of this series is to offer up-to-date information about important issues in our world.

The Refugee Crisis examines the plight of refugees and asylum seekers in the UK and around the world.

The information comes from a wide variety of sources and includes:
Government reports and statistics
Newspaper reports and features
Magazine articles and surveys
Literature from lobby groups
and charitable organisations.

It is hoped that, as you read about the many aspects of the issues explored in this book, you will critically evaluate the information presented. It is important that you decide whether you are being presented with facts or opinions. Does the writer give a biased or an unbiased report? If an opinion is being expressed, do you agree with the writer?

The Refugee Crisis offers a useful starting-point for those who need convenient access to information about the many issues involved. However, it is only a starting-point. At the back of the book is a list of organisations which you may want to contact for further information.

*****

Refugees around the world

Information from the Refugee Council

In today's world there are over 12 million refugees with legal status. They are ordinary people who have fled from their own countries because of war, or because their religion, political beliefs, ethnic group or way of life puts them in danger of arrest, torture or death.

Another 25 to 30 million people have fled from their homes because their lives are in danger, but have gone into hiding in their home country. This group of people are called displaced people. They have fled from their homes for the same reasons as refugees. Their needs are the same as refugees. The difference between displaced people and refugees is that refugees have left their own countries.

One person out of every 115 people alive today is a refugee or displaced person. There are refugees living in every country in the world, but today most refugees live in the poorer countries of Africa or Asia. Most of the world's displaced people also live in these countries.

Refugees in Europe

About 5 million refugees are living in western Europe. They have fled from many different countries.

Bosnia and Croatia

More than 3.5 million people fled from their homes between 1991 and 1995 during the fighting in Croatia and Bosnia. Today there are still 600,000 Bosnian refugees. Most of them live in Croatia and in Germany. Another 840,000 Bosnian people are homeless in Bosnia.

Kosovo

Ethnic Albanians from Kosovo, part of the Federal Republic of Yugoslavia, have been seeking sanctuary in the UK and other European countries in large numbers since the early 1990s

as a result of the Yugoslav government's brutal policies to remove Kosovo's autonomy. Evidence of massacres of civilians increased in the late 1990s, attempted peace talks collapsed in 1999, and in Spring 1999, NATO carried out its threat of air strikes against the Yugoslav government. During the conflict, around 850,000 Kosovan Albanians fled a concerted campaign of ethnic cleansing by Serb forces. A peace agreement was signed in June 1999, NATO forces went into Kosovo, and in the following weeks almost 90 per cent of those who had fled returned. The situation in some areas of the region remains volatile; non-Albanians and, increasingly, moderate Kosovan Albanians, are subject to harassment and murder.

Fighting in the Caucasus

Wars are being fought in southern Russia, Armenia, Azerbaijan and Georgia. In this part of the world, known as the Caucasus, there are 1,720,000 refugees and displaced people. The push by Chechnya for independence from Russia has culminated in heavy military attacks by Russian troops towards the end of 1999. As a result, a minimum of 300,000 Chechens either fled Chechnya or are displaced within Chechnya unable to leave.

The Palestinians: refugees for 50 years

There are over 4,250,000 Palestinian refugees living in the Gaza Strip, the West Bank, Jordan, Syria and Lebanon. They fled their homes after Arab/Israeli wars in 1948/49, 1967, 1982 and after the Gulf War of 1991.

Kurdish refugees

Over 20 million Kurdish people live in the Middle East. In Turkey, Iran and Iraq, the Kurds have faced many

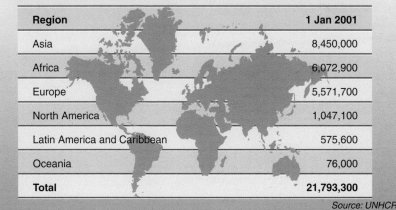

Persons of concern

UNHCR helps the world's uprooted peoples by providing them with basic necessities such as shelter, food, water and medicine in emergencies and seeking long-term solutions, including voluntary return to their homes or beginning afresh in new countries. In more than five decades, the agency has helped an estimated 50 million people restart their lives. Today, a staff of around 5,000 people in more than 120 countries continues to help an estimated 22 million people.

Estimated number of persons of concern who fall under the mandate of UNHCR

Region	1 Jan 2001
Asia	8,450,000
Africa	6,072,900
Europe	5,571,700
North America	1,047,100
Latin America and Caribbean	575,600
Oceania	76,000
Total	21,793,300

Source: UNHCR

dangers since the 1920s. Today there are over 400,000 Kurdish refugees in Europe and the Middle East. Another 1,100,000 Kurds have had their homes destroyed in Turkey and Iraq.

In danger in Colombia

Fighting in Colombia has caused over 1 million people to flee from their homes. Most of them have gone into hiding in other parts of Colombia.

Afghan refugees

There has been a war in Afghanistan since 1979 and many refugees have fled from their homes. Today 1,400,000 Afghan refugees live in Iran and 1,200,000 Afghan refugees live in Pakistan. Another 300,000 Afghan people are displaced in their own country.

Sri Lankan Tamil refugees

Tamil people in Sri Lanka are an ethnic minority group. Some Tamils want an independent country and have been fighting for this. Ordinary people have been caught up in the war between Tamil fighters and the Sri Lankan army. Over 170,000 people are refugees in India. Other refugees have fled to European countries and Canada. Another 800,000 Tamil people have fled their homes but stayed in Sri Lanka.

Bhutan

Over 100,000 Nepali-speaking people have fled from their homes in Bhutan and are now living as refugees in Nepal. They have fled from their homes after the government of Bhutan took away their rights to live in their country and tried to force them to wear Bhutanese national costume.

Refugees in West Africa

War in Sierra Leone and Liberia has caused more than 1,775,000 million people to flee from their homes.

Angola

There has been war in Angola for many years. Today there are 220,000 Angolan refugees living in other African countries. Another 1,200,000 Angolan people are displaced in their own country.

Congo (formerly known as Zaire)

Over 200,000 refugees have fled to other countries in Africa and in Europe to escape fighting. Some refugees from Congo-Zaire have opposed the government and risk being arrested or killed for their political beliefs.

Fighting and danger in Sudan

There has been war in southern Sudan since the 1950s. Today the Sudanese government also imprisons those people who oppose it. As a result over 350,000 people have fled as refugees. Another four million people have fled from their homes and moved to another part of Sudan.

War in Somalia

Refugees have been fleeing fighting in Somalia since 1988. Today there are over 665,000 Somali refugees in Africa and Europe. Another 200,000 Somali people are displaced in their own country.

Going home to Eritrea

The war in Eritrea ended in 1991. But fighting had destroyed houses, roads and schools and it was very difficult for refugees to return home. Now Eritrean refugees are starting to return home from the Sudan. Another 320,000 refugees are still living in the Sudan.

The emergency in Rwanda and Burundi

In Rwanda and Burundi there has been conflict between Hutu and Tutsi people for many years. In June 1994, about 1,500,000 people, mostly Tutsi, were murdered in Rwanda. In Burundi, both Tutsi and Hutu people are being killed by racists. Today over 870,000 people have fled from their homes in Rwanda and Burundi.

Refugees have also fled from many other countries, including Algeria, Bangladesh, China (Tibet), Guatemala, India, Iraq, Iran, Kenya, Mali, Mauritania, Myanmar (Burma), and Western Sahara.

• The above information is an extract from the Refugee Council's web site: www.refugeecouncil.org.uk Alternatively, see page 41 for their address details.

© Refugee Council

Total asylum applications in Europe

This table represents spontaneous new applications lodged in these states during 1999 and 2000, although the figure for Austria may include some second applications (made by persons who had already lodged applications in previous years). The figures for Lithuania and the UK are for cases (i.e. an asylum seeker plus any dependants with him), not individuals. UNHCR estimates that, in the UK, a case comprises on average 1.28 persons. Danish statistics do not include applicants refused on third country grounds.

Country	1999	2000	Variation +/- (%)
Austria	20,096	18,284	-9.0
Belgium	35,778	42,691	+19.3
Bulgaria	1,349	1,755	+30.1
Czech Republic	7,214	8,787	+21.8
Denmark	6,530	10,347	+58.5
Finland	3,106	3,170	+2.0
France	30,830	38,747	+25.0
Germany	95,113	78,564	-17.4
Greece	1,528	3,083	+101.8
Hungary*	11,499	7,799	-32.2
Ireland	7,720*	10,938	+42.0
Italy	34,300	14,000	-59.2
Lithuania	138	199	+44.0
Luxembourg	2,812	628	-78.4
Netherlands	39,299	42,898	+11.7
Norway	10,160	10,842	+6.0
Poland	2,858	4,396	+53.8
Portugal	271	202	-25.2
Romania*	1,665	1,362	-18.2
Slovakia	1,313	1,556	+18.5
Spain	8,405	7,926	-5.7
Sweden	11,231	16,381	+45.9
Switzerland	46,068	17,611	-61.8
United Kingdom	71,160	76,040	+6.9
Total	451,409	428,417	-5.1

| * Figures supplied by UNHCR | Source: ECRE Country Reports for 2000 |

Why do people become refugees?

Information from CAFOD

How do you define a refugee?

In 1951, the United Nations defined a refugee as:

'A person who, owing to a well-founded fear of being persecuted for reasons of race, religion, nationality, membership of a particular social group or political opinion, is outside the country of his/her origin, and is unwilling or . . . unable to return to it.'

Millions of people escape from persecution but do not leave their own country. Others are forced to leave because of environmental de-gradation and may be just as in need of support as those who fall under the UN definition. In a sense, anyone who has been forced to flee is a refugee.

Why do people become refugees?

War

Conflict between two countries, or between different groups in the same country, may drive people from their homes. Seventeen years of civil war in Mozambique between 1975 and 1992 forced 1.5 million people to flee to safety in neighbouring countries.

Environmental disasters

Drought, flooding, and deforestation force people to abandon their homes. Global warming has turned farming land into desert in many parts of the world, leaving people with no choice but to migrate to a new region. In 1980 alone 200,00 sq. kms of arable land were lost in Africa to the advance of the Sahara desert.

Repression

Some governments crush any opposition in order to keep their hold on power. This results in people fleeing from persecution, fear of death and torture. Kurdish people have suffered terrible repression in Iraq, forcing them to seek refuge in nearby countries like Turkey and Iran.

What are the needs of refugees?

Asylum

Refugees need protection and a safe place to live, which means that they need to be offered asylum. They also need basic provisions such as food, clothing and medical care. After that, it is important that refugees are encouraged to regain their independence and their confidence in a new situation.

Long-term solutions are not quite so simple. There are three main options:

Repatriation

Some refugees are soon able to return to their own country when the conflicts there have been resolved. However, under international law they should not be forced to return if there is any further danger.

Local integration

Local integration into refugee camps is a temporary solution until either the situation in their own country improves or they are given permanent status and can settle down in the new country. But spending several years in a camp can be very demoralising for refugees, who may be forced to become dependent on welfare and lose their self-confidence and self-respect.

Full integration

Full integration into another country, with the rights of full citizenship, brings some kind of long-term answer to the dilemmas of a person forced to flee from their homeland. Help in adjusting to the new culture is vital along with education, literacy and language classes, counselling and advice.

International aid

The United Nations High Commission for Refugees was set up in 1951 by the United Nations and is the biggest organisation working to protect refugees and asylum seekers. It has three main aims: first, to make sure that governments follow the rules of international law which relate to refugees; second, to work with other organisations to ensure that aid reaches refugees; third, to try to find long-term solutions for refugees, helping them to return home if possible and if not to settle in a new country.

Contributing to society

Throughout history, refugees have enriched the culture, society and economy of the countries where they have found safety. Newspaper stories have sometimes suggested that refugees are really nothing more than bogus asylum-seekers trying to benefit from social security payments. In fact, refugees contribute as much as they receive from their new home. They bring new expertise and great resourcefulness, as well as a breadth of experience which most people never acquire. They also develop the host country's culture through their involvement in its music, art, drama and cuisine.

Albert Einstein came to the United States as a refugee and became one of the most famous scientists in the world.

'The fact that 15 Nobel Prizes have been won by refugees who found asylum in Britain is a dramatic illustration of refugees' potential to enrich and contribute to act'
(A.Philips: *Employment as a key to settlement.*)

What CAFOD is doing . . .

CAFOD works with refugees and displaced people in many parts of the world. Programmes cover a wide ranges of needs, from the provision of immediate relief to skills training and lobbying. Working through Church partners, CAFOD is able to strengthen local communities receiving new numbers of refugees. For those who have little hope of

Karma was born in Sri Lanka. When civil war broke out the village where she lived was attacked and her home was destroyed. She and her mother escaped. They paid an agent to arrange airline tickets and travel documents, and a short time later they left for Britain. In London, they were taken to a Detention Centre but a refugee action group was able to secure 'temporary admission' for them into the UK. Karma and her mum are now applying for asylum. They have very little, but at least they should be safe now.

returning home, the agency supports programmes which help them to become self-sufficient in their new country. In the UK, CAFOD works through education programmes in schools, youth groups, and parishes to encourage people to take action in their local community in response to global issues like this.

What you can do . . .

1. Get involved in CAFOD's Refugee Campaign. This is a way of finding out why people become refugees, and an opportunity to take action with others all over England and Wales to tackle the causes. Information and materials available from the Campaign Office, CAFOD, Romero Close, Stockwell Road, London SW9 9TY.

2. Find out more about refugees in Britain, and particularly in your local area, by contacting the Refugee Council, 3 Bondway, London, SW9 ISJ.

3. Support fundraising activities to enable CAFOD to continue its work with refugees and displaced people.

4. Look at your local community or your school and see if there are ways you could welcome new people and help them integrate more easily. You could make a guide to your local area or school, or invite them home.

• The above information is an extract from the CAFOD's web site which can be found at www.cafod.org.uk Alternatively, see page 41 for their address details.

CAFOD – The Catholic Agency for Overseas Development

Frequently asked questions

Information from the Refugee Council

There are many misconceptions about asylum seekers in the UK. A *Reader's Digest* Mori poll carried out in 2000 revealed the lack of understanding surrounding this issue. On average people grossly overestimated the amount of money that asylum seekers are given, believing it to be on average £113 a week. In fact, single asylum seekers receive £36.54 in vouchers – just 70% of basic income support. It is not always easy to get accurate answers about asylum, a hotly debated and often emotive issue, one which is not always truthfully represented by the press and is susceptible to political spin. Here are answers to just some of the questions the Refugee Council is often asked.

Who is a refugee?

Under international law, the word 'refugee' has a very precise meaning, as set out in the 1951 United Nations Convention Relating to Refugees. In the Convention, a refugee is defined as someone who:

- has a well-founded fear of persecution for reasons of race, religion, nationality, membership of a particular social group, or political opinion;
- is outside the country they belong to or normally reside in, and
- is unable or unwilling to return home for fear of persecution.

The Convention was drafted in the context of the millions of refugees in post-war Europe, and only applied to European nationals. In 1967, a UN protocol extended the convention to cover any person, anywhere in the world, at any time. The UK, along with over 130 other countries, is a signatory to the Convention and its protocol. These two documents remain the foundation of refugee law today, committing signatories to certain obligations. However, the interpretation of these international

instruments varies from country to country.

Whilst someone is waiting for their application to be considered by the Government, they are known as an 'asylum seeker'.

Some refugees have fled from countries where they may have been persecuted simply for being a member of a religious or ethnic group. Some have taken a deliberate stand against an oppressive government; others have already been in the UK as visitors or students when political changes in their home country made it extremely dangerous for them to return.

Where do Britain's asylum seekers come from?

Asylum seekers come to the UK from the world's trouble spots. The numbers of asylum seekers arriving in the UK inevitably reflect the international situation at any one time. In 2000, the highest number of asylum applications came from nationals of Iraq (9% of applications), Sri Lanka (8%), the Federal Republic of Yugoslavia (7%), Afghanistan (7%), Iran (7%) and Somalia (6%).

Why should the UK support asylum seekers and refugees?

Like all other signatories of the 1951 Convention, the UK has an obligation under international law to protect people fleeing persecution. The UK has also committed itself to the principles of the Universal Declaration of Human Rights (1948), which includes the right to seek and enjoy asylum in other countries. As a signatory to the Convention, the UK is responsible for guaranteeing that those with refugee status enjoy equal rights to UK citizens.

Why do all asylum seekers come to the UK?

They don't. The Home Office received 76,040 applications for asylum in 2000; this may seem like a lot, but not when compared with the number of asylum seekers (nearly 900,000) and refugees (over 12 million) worldwide. In fact, most people seek asylum in neighbouring countries. There are nearly two million Afghan refugees in Iran and 1.2 million in Pakistan. Guinea, which has a population of under 7 million, supports 500,000 refugees from Sierra Leone and Liberia – a ratio 50 times that of the UK.* Some of the poorest countries in the world support the largest numbers of refugees.

* All figures from the United Nations High Commissioner for Refugees (UNHCR)

According to a European Commission-funded study, *Asylum Migration to the European Union: Patterns of Origin and Destination* (1997), most asylum seekers don't choose their country of asylum: where they end up depends mostly on how quickly they fled and by what means. Of those who are able to choose, important factors are those such as existing communities, colonial bonds and knowledge of language. Only a small group are influenced by economic factors, and most have little previous knowledge of regulations about work or welfare support in the UK.

Is the UK a 'soft touch' compared with the rest of Europe?

No. According to the United Nations High Commissioner for Refugees, the UK ranks only 7th out of 15 European Union countries in terms of asylum applicants per 1000 inhabitants.

In fact, asylum seekers find it increasingly difficult to reach the UK's shores. The UK Government imposes visa restrictions on countries which produce large numbers of asylum seekers, who are unable to claim asylum from their own country. Transport companies are now also fined for bringing people into the UK without the right documents.

Life in the UK has become increasingly harsh for asylum seekers. The Immigration and Asylum Act 1999 removed asylum seekers from the welfare benefits system. The act set up a support system where the new Home Office National Asylum Support Service (NASS) is responsible for the welfare of asylum seekers. Asylum seekers are now entitled to vouchers worth 70% of basic income support if they can prove they have no other means of support. Only £10 of the weekly voucher allowance can be exchanged for cash.

Why don't asylum seekers stay in France or other European countries?

Many asylum seekers do seek asylum in other European countries. If we compare the European Union countries, the UK ranks 7th in terms of applicants per 1000 inhabitants, according to the United Nations High Commissioner for Refugees.

The fact that someone has travelled to the UK through another European country does not mean their asylum claim is less credible. Unfortunately, some democratic European countries may not be as safe for asylum seekers as we think. Different countries have different interpretations of the United Nations Convention Relating to Refugees,

which means that one may offer protection where another refuses an application. France, for example, may not necessarily grant refugee status to Algerian asylum seekers, escaping violence from militant groups, as France does not offer protection to those fleeing persecution from any group acting independently of the government.

Aren't all asylum seekers 'bogus'?

On initial decisions alone, the Home Office found 21,565 (31%) asylum seekers to be in need of protection (Refugee Status and Exceptional Leave to Remain) in 2000.

Many refusals are overturned at appeal by adjudicators: 18% in 2000. Some decisions are overturned at the next stage (the Immigration Appeals Tribunal); the exact number is not available from the Home Office.

Is the asylum process as fair as people say it is?

The asylum determination system presents a number of obstacles for asylum seekers in the UK:

- Some asylum seekers are interviewed as soon as they arrive in the UK. This means they have no opportunity to get legal advice. They may also be in a state of shock or trauma due to recent experiences.
- Asylum seekers who are not interviewed immediately are given a 19-page Statement of Evidence Form (SEF) to complete

within ten working days of receipt. The SEF is very complicated and can only be completed in English. It is often difficult for asylum seekers to find interpreters to help them complete the form. If they fail to return the SEF, the Home Office will not even look at the merits of their asylum claim, and refuse their application outright. At the end of 2000, around 35% of asylum applications were refused in this way. This means that an asylum seeker may be returned to their country of origin to face persecution, even death, without having their case properly considered.

- Asylum seekers need legal advice and representation to adequately present their asylum case. However, there are simply not enough legal advisers available to do this work. A recent Law Society survey shows that most asylum seekers have difficulty finding a legal adviser to help them. To make matters worse, newly-arrived asylum seekers are being dispersed to accommodation outside London, where it can be extremely difficult to access good legal advice on asylum.
- The Home Office routinely decides that some asylum applications are without merit. This could be because the asylum seeker's country of origin is deemed to be safe. These cases

are fast-tracked and may then have limited appeal rights. Such cases are also more likely to be detained.

How could the asylum system be fairer?

The Refugee Council believes that a fair asylum determination should ensure:

- That each asylum application is examined on its own merit, as laid out in the 1951 United Nations Convention Relating to Refugees.
- That asylum seekers have adequate time and means to complete all necessary documentation, and access to legal advice and interpreters.
- That those making decisions on asylum applications are properly trained and well-informed about the situations in asylum seekers' countries of origin.
- That all unsuccessful applicants have equal access to the appeals procedure with reasonable time limits.

Are asylum seekers illegal immigrants?

No. Under the 1951 United Nations Convention Relating to Refugees anyone has a legal right to seek asylum in the UK and remain in the country for the duration of their asylum claim.

Why do asylum seekers use smugglers?

Current laws in the UK make it extremely difficult for individuals to legally access the asylum system. For example:

- visa restrictions have been imposed on many refugee-producing countries even though it is difficult for people fleeing persecution to obtain necessary documentation. Simply applying for a passport in their home country may put their lives at risk, let alone visiting a foreign embassy to apply for a visa.
- EU governments have introduced strict controls at ports and airports, as well as fines on all of those found bringing asylum seekers into the UK without the correct documents.

The fact that someone has arrived here illegally does not undermine the credibility of their claim – the reverse is often true. Desperate people fleeing persecution may need to resort to such measures in order to seek asylum, as restrictive immigration controls bar them from entering legally. In doing so, they put themselves at serious risk of extortion, exploitation and physical harm.

Asylum seekers don't contribute anything, do they?

Refugees and asylum seekers have a huge variety of skills and, given the opportunity to work, make significant contributions to the economy and culture of the UK. A recent Home Office report shows that people born outside the UK, including asylum seekers, contribute 10% more to the economy in taxes and national insurance than they consume in benefits and public services – equivalent to a boost to the economy of £2.6 billion in 1998/99.

Are asylum seekers taking our jobs?

In a recent speech to the Institute of Public Policy Research, Immigration Minister Barbara Roche identified major labour shortfalls in key industries such as IT, health and agriculture. There is therefore a great need for the skills asylum seekers and refugees have to offer.

Asylum seekers are not allowed to work for the first six months of their asylum application. Those who are able to work face serious difficulties in finding work, including lack of information about employment and training, limited English, little work experience in the UK, and lack of recognition of qualifications

---

Refugees and asylum seekers have a huge variety of skills and, given the opportunity to work, make significant contributions to the economy and culture of the UK

---

obtained at home. The Home Office has recognised the qualifications and experiences that refugees have to offer and concluded that a failure to use their skills means a substantial loss to the country as a whole.

Whatever the economic benefits, saving people from persecution should never be a matter of economic gain. The right to seek and enjoy asylum is a fundamental human right and the UK is obliged to protect people fleeing persecution under the 1951 Convention Relating to Refugees.

Don't asylum seekers take much-needed council homes?

Asylum seekers are not entitled to be included on council housing lists. Accommodation is provided by the National Asylum Support Service (NASS), a Home Office department. It is only offered outside London and the South-East and asylum seekers have no choice over their destination.

When an asylum seeker is given refugee status or exceptional leave to remain they are entitled to apply for council housing if they are in priority need, like everyone else in the UK.

Do asylum seekers get more money than pensioners?

No. Asylum seekers are only entitled to the equivalent of 70% of basic income support. A single asylum seeker receives £36.54 a week paid in vouchers, of which £10 can be exchanged into cash. Currently the level of income support (minimum income guarantee) for older people is £92.15 and the basic state pension is £72.50 per week.

What happens when asylum seekers' applications are successful?

When asylum seekers are recognised as refugees under the 1951 United Nations Convention Relating to Refugees they have exactly the same rights as UK citizens.

- The above information is an extract from the Refugee Council's web site which can be found at www.refugeecouncil.org.uk Alternatively, see page 41 for their address details.

© Refugee Council

Who are refugees?

Information from Refugee Action

Many people in the UK think that refugees are people fleeing war, oppressive regimes, famine or disasters. The United Nations defines a refugee as someone who has: 'a well-founded fear of persecution for reasons of race, religion, nationality, membership of a particular social group, or political opinion; is outside the country they normally reside in and is unable or unwilling to return home for fear of persecution' (1951 UN Convention).

There are 12 million refugees worldwide. Most seek asylum in neighbouring countries – for instance, there are 2 million Afghan refugees in Iran. Some of the poorest countries support some of the largest numbers of displaced people.

Last year there were just 76,040 applications for asylum in the UK.

They are among some of the most vulnerable people in our communities: they have fled unimaginable persecution, and have often been the victims of violence. Forced to flee, their lives have been turned upside down. They come to the UK in search of safety and sanctuary. Refugee Action is committed to helping them build a new life here.

Refugees' stories

Shima's story

When Shima arrived on a boat at Liverpool docks in September, she was so ill she was taken to Liverpool Women's Hospital by ambulance. It was her 24th birthday and she was seven months pregnant. Shima had hardly eaten during the long voyage from Nigeria and was desperately ill. In the five days she spent in hospital, Shima sobbed continually: she was alone, confused and terrified of what would happen to her. She was discharged from hospital, put in a taxi and sent to Refugee Action's local office, clutching a prayer book and her best dress.

Shima's journey began in Jos, Nigeria. At home with her parents, brother and sister, Shima was studying English, earning some money by weaving hair, and preparing for the birth of her first child. Inter-religious violence had erupted in the region earlier this year but since the conflict had not reached their town, Shima's husband left for work as usual that morning. Hours later an angry mob attacked the house. No one had time to pack or plan; they fled. 'I was just running for my life and praying!' she explains. 'It was a terrible day.' Heavily pregnant but too afraid to return home, Shima spent four days in hiding. What happened next remains a confusing blur. 'I just started walking,' she says. 'It was a tiny road and I was just walking, walking. Then there were no houses, just rocks at the edge of the sea. And the water was freezing. I was cold.'

Once out of hospital in Liverpool, Refugee Action arranged for Shima to get legal advice on her claim for asylum, and financial support and temporary accommodation from the National Asylum Support System. Shima has found it almost impossible to settle in her temporary home whilst she waits for a decision from the Home Office on her claim. She spends most of the time restlessly worrying that her family in Nigeria were killed.

Shima's only visitor is Sarah, a volunteer from the Cara Befriending Scheme in Liverpool. Sarah remembers taking a telephone call from one of the other women in Shima's house to say that she had gone into labour. After a difficult and painful time, the baby was eventually born by caesarean section and Sarah was on hand to see Shima give birth. Back at home Shima's landlord is doing all he can to make her temporary stay comfortable but her room is on the first floor and is far from ideal for new mum and baby. When the heating and hot water failed last week Shima had the painful task of carrying hot water upstairs, not helping heal her caesarean scar.

Shima has no contact with other Nigerians in Liverpool. This isolation, coupled with the fact that there is no news of her family in Nigeria, makes life especially hard at a time when any new parent wants to share their happiness with friends and family. Whilst life is made more bearable by her befriender, it is an anxious time with no news from home and uncertainty about her future here. It is far from the kind of start a new family expects. But at least Shima's welcome to the UK has been arguably better than most.

Sharmila's story

'I found out I was pregnant soon after I arrived in the UK, from Somalia, with my two small children. The friend who supported us for six months could not afford to keep us all, so I went to Refugee Action for help. They helped me find somewhere to live but on the first day in our new home a young man threw stones at the windows and shouted abuse. Every time I went out he shouted at me, and let his dogs loose at me. My baby was almost due, so I was very frightened and the children were scared. My children are very young, my daughter is 6 and my son just 3. One morning I found abuse written on my window. Then after I had been there for one week, a big stone was thrown through my window. Four boys were outside shouting and making noises. One shouted through the letterbox. My son was very scared and even though we are in a different house now he is too afraid to go upstairs on his own.'

• The above information is an extract from Refugee Action's web site which can be found at www.refugee-action.org

© Refugee Action 2001

Asylum in the UK

Fairer, faster and firmer – an introduction to the UK asylum system

The United Kingdom has a proud tradition of providing a safe haven for genuine refugees. The UK Government is determined to ensure that genuine refugees are properly protected and that there is no incentive for people who wish to migrate for other reasons to misuse asylum procedures.

The UK is a signatory to the 1951 UN Convention relating to the Status of Refugees and its 1967 Protocol. All applications for asylum made at UK ports of entry or within the country are considered in accordance with the obligations under the Convention. The Convention states that a refugee is a person who 'owing to a well-founded fear of being persecuted for reasons of race, religion, nationality, membership of a particular social group, or political opinion, is outside the country of his nationality, and is unable or, owing to such fear, is unwilling to avail himself of the protection of that country'.

As set out in the Immigration and Asylum White Paper published in July 1998, the Government is committed to delivering a fairer, faster and firmer immigration and asylum system. Fundamental to the White Paper strategy is the need to modernise asylum procedures and deliver faster decisions. The Government aims to deliver most initial asylum decisions within two months and most appeals within a further four months, from April 2001.

The Immigration and Asylum Act 1999 implements many of the White Paper changes required to provide protection for those in genuine need whilst dealing quickly and firmly with unfounded applicants.

The main features of the UK asylum system are as follows:
- All claims receive a fair hearing.
- Fast-track processes mean that some claims (and subsequent appeals) are dealt with in about four weeks. Claimants may be detained for all or part of that time.
- All claimants have a responsibility to co-operate with the authorities considering their claim. They must:
- Tell the truth about their circumstances;
- Obey the law. It is a criminal offence to submit a claim involving deception, the maximum penalty for which is two years' imprisonment;
- Keep in regular contact with the authorities considering their claim;
- Leave the country if their claim is ultimately rejected.
- Support is provided to those asylum seekers who are destitute. Accommodation is provided on a 'no choice' basis in parts of the UK where there is less pressure on accommodation than in London and other parts of the South-East. Asylum seekers are given vouchers for food and other goods, and £10 cash per week. The dispersal system and provision of vouchers is organised by the new National Asylum Support Service (NASS).
- Some claimants are removed to another EU member state in order to pursue their claim there, if that member state is responsible for the claim under the terms of the Dublin Convention. Some other claimants are removed in order to pursue their claim in a safe country outside the European Union.
- Asylum seekers can appeal against refusal of their application or against the grant of exceptional leave to remain rather than refugee status. There is now a single 'one stop' right of appeal.
- The Government is also introducing a scheme to regulate immigration advisers to prevent asylum seekers being exploited by unscrupulous or incompetent advisers.
- Those who are unsuccessful on appeal will be required to leave the UK. If necessary, they will be removed.
- Those who are recognised as refugees will be granted immediate settlement in the UK and will be helped to build a new life.

- The above information is an extract from the Home Office web site which can be found at www.homeoffice.gov.uk

Asylum myths

Information from Oxfam

Introduction

Over an eight-week period, starting on 6 March 2000 and ending on 28 April 2000, all weekday news coverage of asylum issues was collected from six Scottish newspapers. The papers were the *Daily Record, Herald, Scotsman, Scottish Daily Express, Scottish Daily Mail,* and the *Scottish Sun*. Each printed article was evaluated by using a number of categories that aimed to quantify key trends in asylum reportage. Each article was classified as either negative, balanced, or positive. Identifying the amount of coverage in each area of the asylum debate made it possible to see what areas the press were focusing on in the debate, and which subject areas generated the most negative and the most positive coverage.

The Press Complaints Commission cautioned newspaper editors in 2000 about 'the danger that inaccurate and misleading reporting may generate an atmosphere of fear and hostility which is not borne out by the facts'.

Over the two-month period of the study, the six newspapers monitored contained a total of 253 articles that were concerned with asylum seekers or asylum issues. The

tone of these articles was classified as follows:

- Positive 21%
- Negative 44%
- Balanced 35%

The repetition of a number of myths about asylum seekers and asylum issues was a major feature of the coverage analysed. Here we outline the facts behind the myths and the most common messages, based on the myths, that were articulated by the press.

The scale of the problem, and questions of eligibility

*Myth: **The number of people applying for asylum in Britain is reaching crisis proportions. Britain is a 'soft touch' and takes more than its fair share of refugees.***

Facts: According to recent figures produced by the United Nations High Commissioner for Refugees, the UK received a total of 76,040

applications for asylum in 2000; this represents a 7 per cent increase on 1999. However, relative to the size of their population, many other European countries take far more asylum seekers than we do per head: Britain ranks seventh out of 15 EU countries in these terms, with 1.66 applications per 1000 people. Belgium ranked highest (4.20 per 1000), with Ireland, the Netherlands, Austria, Denmark, and Sweden all receiving more applications than Britain, relative to the size of their population.[1]

Moreover, it is primarily the poor countries in the South that bear the brunt of refugee movements. There are an estimated 1.8 million refugees in Iran, more than 450,000 in Guinea, and over 400,000 in Tanzania.[2]

Myth: Most asylum seekers come from safe countries.

Facts: The majority of refugees arriving in the UK to seek asylum in recent years have been from the former Yugoslavia, Somalia, Sri Lanka, Afghanistan, Turkey, Iraq, and Iran. These are all countries where there has been serious conflict or where grave abuses of human rights are common.

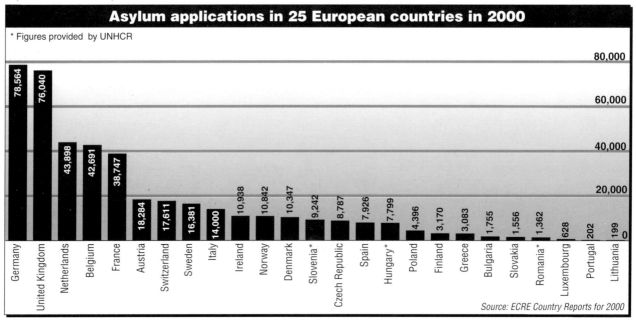

Myth: Only a tiny proportion of refugees are genuine, and the rest are ineligible for asylum.

Facts: Even under the current system of assessing claims for asylum, about which many refugee organisations have expressed concern, around 47 per cent of asylum seekers were found to be in need of protection and were allowed to remain during 1999, and around 22 per cent during 2000, following first decisions. However, this ignores the fact that many refusals are overturned at appeal; in 2000, appeal adjudicators upheld 17 per cent of appeals that came before them.[3]

Furthermore, the past year has seen a dramatic rise in rejections based on technicalities – up from 1,085 in 1999 to 26,635 in 2000. This is because asylum seekers have been given only ten working days to complete and submit a 19-page 'Statement of Evidence form', in which they must outline the basis of their claim. Often without legal help and lacking sufficient English to complete the form properly, their applications are frequently refused on the grounds of 'non-compliance'. In such cases, the validity of their actual claim is therefore not even considered.[4]

Adjudication meetings for asylum claims have also been a cause for concern. For example, notification of meeting dates in London for asylum seekers dispersed to Glasgow has often been given at extremely short notice – in some cases one or two days before the date of the meeting. It takes a further five days for a travel pass to be issued, and if someone fails to attend for the meeting the case is dismissed until appeal.

Finally, there are also some who appear to be rejected unfairly. For example, their application may be turned down for entering the UK with false papers, despite the fact that this may have been the only way to escape persecution in the asylum seeker's country of origin – a reality that is acknowledged under international refugee law (Article 31, 1951 Refugee Convention).

On this basis, there is no justification for routinely attaching the adjective 'bogus' to all those

---

A 'climate of fear' about asylum seekers has been supported by the press, with the use of unsubstantiated claims about the numbers of people claiming asylum in the UK

---

seeking asylum, which does tremendous harm to those legitimately seeking asylum.

Myth: Most asylum seekers are 'economic migrants'.

Facts: There are clear connections between increases in the incidence of human-rights abuses and persecution in particular countries and rises in the numbers of asylum applicants from those countries (as set out in the response above). On the basis of these figures, large numbers of applicants have legitimate grounds for claiming asylum.

It is important, however, to acknowledge that migration is increasing. Given that there are virtually no legal routes for migrants to enter the UK for the purposes of finding work, some clearly do seek to claim asylum in order to gain entry. To reduce this pressure on the asylum system, it is essential that the government should develop a more open policy towards migration, as recently recommended in a Home Office report.[5]

The evidence is growing that the immigration of workers – not only skilled workers but also unskilled labour – does not impair the welfare of British citizens. On the contrary, it stimulates the economy, and thus the prosperity of the indigenous population. Indeed, given an ageing population and an increasingly service-orientated economy, the welfare of the host population, especially elderly citizens, depends on increased immigration of unskilled workers. Furthermore, the evidence suggests that the vast majority of migrants do not wish to settle in the UK, but to work here temporarily in order to send money home to their families.

How the papers handled it

The number of people applying for asylum in the UK was presented in many newspaper articles as a justification for opposing the admission of asylum seekers. Many articles exaggerated both the numbers of people applying for asylum in the UK and the possible negative effects of increased numbers of asylum seekers on State services, such as the health service.

'We also need to recognise that the problem of asylum is only just beginning. As our prosperity continues, pressure to get here will intensify . . . An asylum free-for-all is a time bomb ticking away . . . that could one day explode with terrifying public violence.'
Scottish Daily Mail 13/04/00.

Asylum seekers were frequently presented in terms of numbers: 'flood', 'wave', and 'influx' accounted for 31 per cent of negative keywords found in the coverage monitored. These words appeared almost as frequently in articles rated as balanced and positive as they did in articles rated as negative. Such descriptions dehumanise asylum seekers and shift the focus of the debate away from the reasons why people are seeking asylum in the UK towards how many people are applying for asylum. Hardly any of the articles which discussed the increase in asylum applications in the UK over recent years associated this increase with the world-wide increase in civil war and ethnic conflict seen at the end of the twentieth century. Instead, the increase is primarily discussed with reference to ineligible applications for asylum. Journalists and other commentators often presented Britain as a target for those making unsupported claims for asylum in the hope of a better life. Those found to be ineligible for refugee status are accused of targeting Britain to obtain State benefits and achieve a higher standard of living.

A 'climate of fear' about asylum seekers has been supported by the press, with the use of unsubstantiated claims about the numbers of people claiming asylum in the UK, their motives, and alleged anti-social behaviour among asylum groups. As identified above, the terms 'asylum', 'economic migration', and 'illegal immigration' are often used synonymously, and asylum seekers are presented as a threat to Britons, instead of the highly vulnerable section of society that they are.

> 'Asylum seekers continue to pour into Britain at the rate of 6,500 a month. Thousands more illegal immigrants are pouring over the English Channel undetected. And to the disgust of taxpayers across Britain, the incomers are creaming off the benefits system . . . And in Dover, the huge influx of refugees across the Channel has led to almost nightly street battles, thefts and attacks.'
> Daily Record, 16/03/00.

Asylum applicants found to be ineligible for refugee status in Britain have been labelled 'bogus' by the British press – a derogatory term that was quickly adopted by many politicians. The word 'bogus' accounted for 32 per cent of the negative key words found in the coverage monitored. Forty-seven per cent of articles including the word 'bogus' were rated as negative, but 27 per cent of occurrences were in articles rated as balanced, and the remaining 26 per cent were found in articles rated as positive. The continual use of the word 'bogus' alongside 'asylum seekers' fixes very negative stereotypes in readers' minds and gives the impression that all those who are refused refugee status have tried in some way to cheat their way into the UK.

> 'Senior judges have made a string of absurd rulings – and made Britain the Costa Del Dole for bogus refugees . . . That is why 300,000 refugees have poured into Britain in the past ten years. The vast bulk of them are here illegally. And with wives and children the true figure could be as high as ONE MILLION.'
> The Scottish Sun, 11/04/00.

Many of the monitored articles discussed economic migration. A key aim of UK asylum policy in recent years has been to deter 'economic migrants' from attempting to use the asylum system to enter the UK illegally in order to work and settle,

a fact which has inextricably linked these two distinct actions.

> 'Asylum seekers who are transferred to Scotland will still receive cash handouts of £150 a week, despite the introduction of tough new laws to curb the number of bogus immigrants.'
> Scottish Daily Mail, 27/03/00.

> 'Government plans to clamp down on bogus asylum seekers came into force yesterday . . . lorry drivers will be hit with £2000 fines if they are caught trying to smuggle illegal immigrants into the country'
> Daily Record, 04/04/00.

Highly negative articles that began by discussing the number of people claiming asylum in the UK would often end by asserting that the rise is due solely to increasing numbers of would-be economic migrants. Coverage of economic migration is a highly emotive subject, and almost all of the articles that broached this subject were negative in tone and opinion. Discussion of economic migration in articles that are concerned with asylum is confusing and seems to close down the debate on both subjects.

> 'Doubts were also raised that the Romanians may not be refugees who were genuinely fleeing political or religious persecution, but in fact are economic migrants seeking a better quality of life.'
> Scotsman, 17/03/00.

Not all ineligible applications for asylum can be classed as an attempt at economic migration, as was frequently implied in press coverage.

> 'However, concern grew last night that some of the Polish refugees may not be fleeing from persecution but are economic migrants.'
> Scottish Daily Mail, 31/03/00.

> 'Unfortunately, due to a bungle by the London borough of Wandsworth, many turned out to be "economic migrants" – beggars to the rest of us. Such bogus refugees have to be dealt with swiftly and decisively.'
> Scottish Daily Express, 17/03/00.

References
1 United Nations High Commissioner for Refugees (2001), Asylum Applications Submitted in Europe 2000.
2 US Committee for Refugees, World Refugee Survey 2000.
3 www.homeoffice.gov.uk/rds/pdfs/asy-dec00.pdf
4 If one deletes those refused on grounds of non-compliance from the total number of asylum applications for 2000, 44 per cent of asylum seekers were found to be in need of protection and allowed to remain in 2000; and even more were permitted to stay after they appealed.
5 S. Glover et al. (2001), Migration: an economic and social analysis, Home Office.

• The above information is an extract from Asylum: The Truth behind the Headlines, produced by Oxfam. The report was commissioned by Oxfam's UK Poverty Programme in Scotland. The Poverty Programme would like to thank a number of people who were involved in its production.

The report arose from a serious concern about the quality of press coverage on asylum in Scotland, and the degree to which asylum seekers arriving in the country are badly affected by the negative coverage that they receive in the Scottish press. It aims to explore how this adverse treatment in sections of the press has been instrumental in creating a climate of fear and hostility towards asylum seekers among sections of the Scottish public, and in supporting government policies which increase hardship and suffering among Scotland's asylum community. The report also sets out a range of recommendations to ensure fair and informed reporting of asylum issues in future. For Oxfam's address details see page 41.

© Oxfam

Young refugees in Britain

Information from Children of the Storm

Every year thousands of refugees under the age of 17 claim asylum in the UK; hundreds of them are not accompanied by any family members. Most are innocent victims of political turmoil and civil strife in different parts of the world who have come to Britain because their lives were threatened at home. Unfortunately, young refugees quickly find that life in the UK can be very difficult. Complicated legislation, racial stereotyping and lack of English language are just three obstacles hindering their social development and educational progress.

Under international law, a refugee is someone who owing to a well-founded fear of being persecuted for reasons of race, religion, nationality, membership of a particular social group or political opinion has fled their country of origin to seek asylum elsewhere. Refugees are legally entitled to protection under the 1951 UN Convention Relating to the Status of Refugees; this protection includes access to social service benefits and education in the country in which they have chosen to take asylum. There are over 27 million refugees world-wide, only a tiny percentage of them claiming asylum in the UK.

Although for the purposes of this information we use the term refugee to cover all young asylum seekers regardless of their status, in Britain someone is only classed as a refugee after their claim for asylum has been approved by the Home Office.

> *Constant changes to the law surrounding the rights of asylum seekers to social services do little to foster a young person's sense of security*

While the need for support mechanisms for young refugees is growing, government legislation has cut services and benefits available to refugees. The Asylum and Immigration Act of 1996 took away the entitlement to benefits for large numbers of asylum seekers. As a result, in April 1997, over 2,300 families and 526 unaccompanied children were without access to benefits. Responsibility for provision of their welfare fell to local councils, charities and community groups. Faced with the inadequacy of state benefits, it is becoming increasingly incumbent on the non-governmental sector to fill in the gaps in support that asylum seekers need.

The constant changes to the law surrounding the rights of asylum seekers to social services do little to foster a young person's sense of security. Moreover, the state takes little account of the fact that an unaccompanied 16-year-old may not have the emotional maturity to cope with living alone. Eligibility for benefits depends largely on an individual's circumstances and Children of the Storm is concerned about the inequality of provision for all young people living in the UK.

Support for young refugees in Britain

Key issues facing young refugees in Britain

1. Education

For most young refugees, continuing their education is their greatest wish.

However, many find it very difficult to adapt to the British education system. This is partly caused by the differences between the British system and that found in their native country. In the former Yugoslavia, for example, exams are done on a continuous basis, with presentations given before the class and weekly grades averaged to give a final mark. In Somalia there is a strong oral tradition in education, much of it having its base in Islam. As such, schooling in Britain may appear not only hostile but irrelevant to their needs. Language and cultural differences make integration with their cohorts even more difficult.

2. Community

While integration into British society is useful for making friends etc., it is vital that young refugees, especially those that are unaccompanied, are kept in touch with their home communities. If they are ever to go back to their homeland or to be reunited with their families it is essential that they have knowledge of their native language, culture and religion. Schools will not always be able to help provide the cultural and religious education that is required, therefore it is important to put unaccompanied refugee children in touch with other people who have come to Britain from their country.

3. Health

Malnutrition and post-traumatic stress disorder are just two conditions which refugees may be suffering from on entry to the UK so comprehensive health checks on arrival are necessary. In reality often these checks do not take place, either because the children are too frightened to see a doctor, or because they do not understand what medical treatment they are entitled to or how to access it. Being separated from their families for the first time, young unaccompanied refugees may not have the knowledge necessary to keep themselves healthy. Responsible attitudes towards health and lifestyles are traditionally built within the family environment so without an adult to advise them, unaccompanied youngsters are more likely to fall prey to illness.

4. Shelter

For refugees aged 16-21, finding suitable accommodation can present a big problem. Many landlords will not accept tenants who are dependent on benefits, and most refugees – as they are not entitled to work – are dependent on the small amount which the social services are prepared to pay. In these circumstances, finding housing can be a long and tedious process.

• The above information is an extract from Children of the Storm's web site which can be found at www.cotstorm.demon.co.uk Alternatively, see page 41 for address details.

© *Children of the Storm*

Plight of the lone child refugees

Young asylum seekers often face a harsh welcome

When his mother told him to leave Afghanistan for the West, Akhbar did not question the decision. As a devout Muslim, he had been brought up to obey his parents and he immediately prepared to go to stay with relatives across the border in Pakistan. His father, a journalist in Kabul, had upset the Taliban authorities and been arrested. Akhbar's mother believed it wouldn't be long before they came for her son.

At 14, Akhbar was considered a man in Afghan society and the new head of the household. With his father gone, there would be little chance of Akhbar earning enough to support his family on his own in Afghanistan, but he might just be able to send sufficient home from Europe.

So, two months ago, Akhbar began the long, solo trip to Britain. The relatives in Pakistan found a

By Martin Bright

middle-man to whom they paid the going rate: a £2,000 down-payment and the same again when his family heard he had arrived safely. Akhbar travelled overland hidden in lorries.

Many children arrive with just the clothes they stand up in and a scrap of paper with a telephone number written on it

He is just one of around 400 Afghan children, mainly boys, being looked after by Kent Social Services. Last week the county announced it was responsible for more than 1,200 unaccompanied children seeking asylum in Britain. To cope with the numbers, officials have set up two dedicated reception centres, one for boys aged between 13 and 15, and another for 16- and 17-year-olds. There, the arrivals are given new clothes, medical treatment and counselling if necessary. They also begin English classes.

Very young children and the small number of girls who arrive are found foster homes immediately. But already Kent is cracking under the strain, and has begun to settle some children in neighbouring counties.

By arriving in Britain, boys like Akhbar have fulfilled a filial duty. He told a recent English class: 'I had to come, and now I have my wish. I live in freedom.'

It is difficult to deport refugee children, although it does happen.

The other main group of child refugees, Kosovar Albanians, are almost impossible to send home, because their villages have often been destroyed and they have lost all contact with their parents.

Many children arrive with just the clothes they stand up in and a scrap of paper with a telephone number written on it. In the case of Afghans the number is often of relatives in Pakistan, who can be told they have arrived – triggering the final payments to the people-traffickers.

Some lone children found on lorries have no idea where they are. The first question they ask is often: 'What country is this?' One Somali girl who turned up in Dover had been told she was going to Germany.

This week the Refugee Council and Save the Children will publish a report on 'separated children' in the UK.

Despite Home Office assurances to the contrary, the two organisations have found many examples of youngsters who have ended up in adult accommodation and even some who have been detained in prison.

Many unaccompanied children have been tortured in their own countries. One boy from Cameroon found in a British prison would not touch the doors because the cells in his country had been electrified.

The report will demand that the Government justifies why there is less money for refugee children in local authority care than for British children. Fazil Kawani of the Refugee Council told *The Observer*: 'The Government urgently needs to do some joined-up thinking to ensure that refugee children stop falling through the net. Many of them have experienced or witnessed un-imaginably horrific situations.'

Sandy Bruce-Lockhart, Conservative leader of Kent County Council, questions the idea that all the children are fleeing persecution. Some parents, he says, have made a calculated choice – part humanitarian and part economic – and sent their children for a better life. He believes the UK is being targeted by racketeers.

But Government figures cast doubt on Bruce-Lockhart's warnings about a growing crisis. The number of unaccompanied children seeking asylum was 3,349 in 1999, but dropped last year to 2,733.

Unlike adult asylum seekers, who are dealt with by the Home Office, under-18s are the responsibility of the local authority under the Children Act. There is no question of them being included in the Government's dispersal system, and they are rarely sent home. For as long as they come, Kent will have to look after them.

• This article first appeared in *The Observer*, 12 August 2001.

© *Guardian Newspapers Limited 2001*

Young refugees

Who, where and why?

What image of refugees do people carry around in their minds? A long snaking trail of malnourished women and children walking through the dust to a refugee camp in Africa? Perhaps a motorised convoy of families, with as many household effects as they can rescue, fleeing conflict in one of the world's many war zones?

How about this – a ten-year-old girl and her 12-year-old brother dropped from a lorry, on their own, outside a motorway service station on the M6?

It is true that – numerically – the first two groups are much larger and the international community needs to address these problems urgently. But in the UK the plight of young refugees (also known as unaccompanied minors, or separated children) also needs attention.

Vulnerable to exploitation

It is really hard to get visas to leave or

enter a country. Even to board a plane or ship requires documentation that many would-be travellers just don't have.

For those suffering persecution and in fear of their lives the only way to escape may be to turn to criminal operations. Organised networks of people-smugglers who bypass security and 'spirit' passengers away from their home country to what they hope will be a safer or better life. The process is risky, very dangerous to life and very expensive. But when people are desperate, they will do almost anything.

What do young refugees need?

Sometimes the pressure of what they have been through and the uncertainty of the future means that young people cannot settle to anything until they have their refugee status sorted out. Many will have had a very traumatic time, witnessing things no one should ever have to witness, undergoing experiences that they will not and cannot ever forget.

Away from family and friends they can be very isolated. But that means their need and desire for the ordinary, everyday things in life is greater, not less. Many simply want what every other young person wants – normality, a social life, a chance to hang out, do sport, get into music or fashion, pursue education.

A welcome gift

The Red Cross is known for its parcels of high quality rations of food, or the means of basic survival. The things a young child coming to this country alone might appreciate – toys and playthings – are not likely to interest teenagers.

So what would you put in a welcome pack to a young teenage refugee to the UK? What would be useful, friendly gifts? What small luxuries might make a big difference to someone feeling alone, bewildered and desperately short of money?

Why do asylum seekers always come to the UK?

The answer is that they don't. Every country in Europe receives significant numbers of refugees. Per head of population the UK ranks 6th as a receiving country – and just 78th in the world.

In fact most refugees head for nearby developing countries. For instance, even before the current conflict Iran was host to 1.8 million refugees from Afghanistan and Pakistan 1.2 million. The UK had just 76,000 new arrivals last year.

Another problem with the question is that it assumes that refugees want to come to the UK. In reality, they may have had no say in it at all. For many young people, the chances are that their parents, fearful of the life they were leading at home,

made the heart-wrenching decision to send them away to a safer place. Indeed, many people arrive without even knowing where they are.

Five things to think about concerning young refugees

1. The number of separated children applying for asylum in the UK is rising steadily. In 1992 just 109 children applied – but by 1999 that figure was 3,349. Nearly half those who applied in 1999 were from Kosovo.
2. Children have basic rights in this country, as the government signed up to the United Nations Convention on the Rights of the Child. The trouble is – it made an exception. It made a special legal reservation to say that refugee children in the UK are not covered by those rights.
   Some campaigners want this changed. They argue that children have rights because they are children and that we as a society should apply those to everyone – not exclude some because of the circumstances of their lives.
3. It is not a good idea to put pressure on young refugees to talk. Some have experienced really awful events. But that doesn't mean that they will feel better if they spill out all their feelings to a strange but sympathetic coun-

sellor. Much better to wait and respond when trust has built up – which will only happen over time.

4. There have been an unknown number of deaths and injuries to young people – suffocating in lorries, drowning while trying to swim ashore, or crushed by the landing gear of planes. Some of the 58 Chinese people found dead in the back of a lorry arriving at Dover were young adults.
5. Here are some prices charged by agents and traffickers. They are only estimated from reports in July 2000, converted into pounds sterling.
   By lorry from Turkey to the UK – £2,000 to £4,000
   By plane from Brazzaville, Congo to Paris – £190 to £280.
   From Sri Lanka to France via Russia or Italy – £2,800 to £3,800
   From Kosovo to Germany – £950
   By small boat from Albania to Italy – £2.30
   From Afghanistan to the UK – £4,000 to £5,000.

Figures supplied by Save the Children.

• From *Reducation*, the magazine produced for the Youth and Schools Unit of the British Red Cross.

The British Red Cross cares for people in crisis in local communities throughout the British Isles and overseas as part of the International Red Cross and Red Crescent Movement.

You can contact them at British Red Cross, 9 Grosvenor Cresent, London, SW1X 7EJ. Tel: 020 7235 5454. Fax: 020 7245 6315. E-mail: information@redcross.org.uk or visit their web site at www.redcross.org.uk
© British Red Cross

The Red Cross is known for its parcels of high quality rations of food, or the means of basic survival

---

Asylum-seekers

Information from Save the Children

People who have been forced from their homes by conflict and danger may have to escape to a foreign country to find a safe place to live. When they ask the government of another country to give them a safe haven as refugees, they are called asylum-seekers. Asylum is another word for 'refuge' or 'sanctuary'. Once their asylum application is officially accepted, they can get special protection under international law as refugees. (A refugee is someone who flees to another country to avoid being tortured, persecuted or killed.)

> *'I was happy in my country, but then the war started and I saw lots of people die.'*

Children who seek asylum in the UK are among the most vulnerable young people in the country, because of what they've already been through and the new worries they face here. Some will have lost their relatives in war. Others may have seen people being tortured or killed. They may have lost their homes, schools, friends and everything that is important to them. The journey to the UK itself may have been traumatic.

Once they get to the UK, the problems mount up. They may not know anybody, have little or no money and nowhere decent to live. If they can't speak English, they'll find it especially hard to survive. Doctors may be unwilling to accept them and some have had difficulty getting a place in school. The chance to continue their education is very important for asylum-seekers, because school may be the only stable and 'normal' part of their lives. 'School gives you a lot of chances to be something in the future,' says Maryam, a young woman from Afghanistan.

Asylum-seekers may get bullied or called names by people who don't understand why they're here. Some children who are seeking asylum have

 **Save the Children**

been physically attacked by racists. Others may even be placed in detention centres, perhaps because they have had to travel on false passports which say they are older than they actually are. Some children are detained with their families for seven days when they arrive in the country while their asylum applications are processed.

Children can seek asylum on their own, as well as with their families. If children arrive here without the adults who usually look after them, they are called 'separated'. They may be on their own because the rest of the family didn't manage to escape.

In 1999, nearly 4,000 separated children claimed asylum in the UK. Life in a new country is particularly tough for them. Social services are supposed to look after these children until they turn 18, but many don't get the same quality of care as other children in need. 'I had to find everything on my own,' says Ardian, a young Albanian man from Kosovo. Ahmed had to leave his family behind when he fled Afghanistan and now lives with an English foster family in Sheffield. He's tortured by his memories: 'I lost my family and never had any information about

---

Children who seek asylum in the UK are among the most vulnerable young people in the country, because of what they've already been through and the new worries they face here

---

them. My problem is in my heart. I can't think about anything else.'

If people are granted asylum, they are given 'refugee status', which means they can stay in the UK as long as they like. Or they may be allowed to stay here for a fixed length of time; this is called 'exceptional leave to remain'. Being denied asylum can mean deportation.

As if that is not enough . . .

Children and young people seeking asylum need all the help they can get. But instead, they get less protection than other children in the UK. A new law – the Immigration and Asylum Act 1999 – makes life more difficult for asylum-seekers by:

- Giving them vouchers instead of welfare benefits. Vouchers are only worth 70-80 per cent of normal income support. (This doesn't affect separated children.)
- Making them move away from London and the South-East to parts of the country where they may not know anyone, where support services are often poor and local people may be hostile to refugees, who are easy to spot because they're forced to shop with vouchers. Moving refugees away from the South-East is supposed to take the pressure off local councils there.

The UK Government justifies this law by saying that giving asylum-seekers vouchers instead of money stops people coming here to take advantage of the welfare system. However, in response to criticism, the Government has now promised to review the voucher system.

This system treats children unequally. Children who are seeking asylum should be seen as children first and foremost, and given the same protection as all other children in the UK.

Save the Children thinks that the UK Government is not honouring its obligations to children. It signed the UN Convention on the

Rights of the Child – an international law which protects everyone under 18 – but reserved the right not to respect what the Convention says about immigration and nationality.

What is Save the Children doing?

We are campaigning for a better deal for children who are refugees and seeking asylum in the UK, as part of our Forgotten Children campaign. We are calling on the UK Government to:

- Remove its reservation to the UN Convention on the Rights of the Child, and give children seeking asylum the same rights to protection and welfare as all other children
- Not put children in detention centres
- Make sure that families seeking asylum get the same benefits as other families on income support
- Make sure that young refugees who are separated from their usual carer get the same help as other young people who are separated from their families. Those leaving care should not be asked to move to another part of the country.

Save the Children has also recently launched the Young Separated Refugees Project. This will highlight the needs of young people who are refugees or seeking asylum, and who have come to the UK without their parents or usual carer.

If you want to find out more about Save the Children's work or to get involved, please visit www.savethechildren.org.uk or contact Education Unit, Save the Children, 17 Grove Lane, London SE5 8RD. Tel: 020 7703 5400. E-mail: yep@scfuk.org.uk

• The above information is from the IntroSheet on *Asylum-seekers* – A guide to today's issues from Save the Children's youth education programme. The IntroSheets are updated regularly on the Save the Children web site: www.savethechildren.org.uk/rightonline, click on the link 'Need Info?' to view the latest information. Alternatively, for additional information and web site addresses of Save the Children see page 41 of this book.

© Save the Children

Running for cover

'Over half the world's refugees are children'

Child refugees

Up to 20 million children have fled their homes because of armed conflict. Many are separated from their families. They are forced to seek safety and survival wherever and however they can – in strange countries, in squalid refugee camps or living rough on city streets. Inside refugee camps, children often find little safety. Unaccompanied girls and boys may be forced into performing sexual favours to get food, water or protection.

Desperately seeking asylum

Many countries – including Australia, Japan, UK and USA – arbitrarily detain children who claim asylum. Only a handful of refugee children reach the UK or other parts of the developed world. But even these few are not guaranteed protection. Many children who claim asylum in the UK are locked up.

In late 1996, a 13-year-old Nigerian girl arrived in the UK with a false passport that said she was 22 years old. Although Immigration Officers accepted that the passport was false, they insisted her age was 22, despite her appearance and her own testimony. So the girl was held in an adult detention centre.

The UK Government made a 'reservation' – an official escape clause – when it ratified the UN Convention on the Rights of the Child – which allows it to treat refugee children differently to other children. This means vulnerable child refugees are not protected by the Convention when they arrive in Britain. The UK's position undermines the Convention – which is meant to protect all children at all times.

Our key messages

Protect children's rights
Children have human rights. Their rights have been increasingly violated in armed conflicts. This is not accidental, but due to the decisions of adults, to target children and to ignore their rights to a childhood. Children need special protection to stop them becoming the victims of human rights violations. Adults can give them this protection.

Defend child refugees
When children escape armed conflict and persecution, our Government should protect them, not imprison them. Children are particularly vulnerable to abuse when they flee armed conflicts and persecution. Our Government should ensure that such children are protected under the UN Convention on the Rights of the Child.

The UK should scrupulously avoid the detention of child asylum seekers. The UK should remove the reservation it has made under Article 22 of the UN Convention of the Rights of the Child, which denies child asylum seekers the Convention's protection.

• The above information is an extract from Amnesty International's web site which can be found at www.amnesty.org.uk Alternatively, see page 41 for their address details.

© Amnesty International

The world of children at a glance

Information from the United Nations High Commission for Refugees (UNHCR)

There are approximately 50 million uprooted people around the world – refugees who have sought safety in another country, and people displaced within their own country. Around half of this displaced population are children.

The United Nations High Commission for Refugees cares for 22.3 million of these people. An estimated 10 million are children under the age of 18.

The majority of people flee their homes because of war. It is estimated that more than two million children were killed in conflict in the last decade. Another six million are believed to have been wounded and one million orphaned.

In recent decades the proportion of war victims who are civilians rather than combatants has leaped from five per cent to more than 90 per cent.

Children in 87 countries live among 60 million land mines. As many as 10,000 per year continue to become victims of mines.

More than 300,000 youths and girls currently are serving as child soldiers around the world. Many are less than 10 years old. Many girl soldiers are forced into different forms of sexual slavery.

The 1989 Convention on the Rights of the Child is the most important legal framework for the protection of children. The Convention has the highest number of state parties of any human rights treaty, being ratified by all countries except the United States and Somalia.

Last year, the UN General Assembly approved two Optional Protocols to the Convention, one on the sale of children and child pornography and another establishing 18 as the minimum age for participation of children in hostilities.

UNHCR has recognised the special needs of refugee children and youngsters uprooted in their own countries. In the last few years, the agency has introduced many new programmes, expanded others and attempted to incorporate all of them into its operations.

Children, whether accompanied by parents or on their own, account for as many as half of all asylum seekers in the industrialised world. In 1996, Canada became the first country with a refugee determination system to issue specific guidelines on children seeking asylum.

Children, whether accompanied by parents or on their own, account for as many as half of all asylum seekers in the industrialised world

---

At any one time there may be up to 100,000 separated children in western Europe alone. As many as 20,000 separated children lodge asylum applications every year in Europe, North America and Oceania.

Between 1994 and 1999, the UN requested $13.5 billion in emergency relief funding, much of it for children. It received less than $9 billion.

The amount of assistance varied dramatically by region. Donors provided the equivalent of 59 US cents per person per day for 3.5 million people in Kosovo and South-eastern Europe in 1999, compared with 13 cents per person per day for 12 million African victims.

AIDS has killed more than 3.8 million children and orphaned another 13 million. In the last five years HIV/AIDS has become the greatest threat to children, especially in countries ravaged by war. In the worst-affected countries, it is estimated that as many as half of today's 15-year-olds will die from the disease.

In 1998 donor countries allocated $300 million to combat AIDS, though an estimated $3 billion was needed.

More than 67,000 children were reunited with their families in Africa's Great Lakes region between 1994-2000, thanks to a global tracing programme organised by humanitarian organisations.

An estimated 45,000 house-holds in Rwanda today are headed by children, 90 per cent of them girls.

School buildings, like teachers and children, have become deliberate targets in war. During the Mozambique conflict in the 1980s-90s, for instance, 45 per cent of schools were destroyed.

If developed countries met an agreed aid target of 0.7 percent of their gross national product, an extra $100 billion would be available to help the world's poorest nations.

An estimated 1.2 billion people worldwide survive on less than $1 per day. Half of them are children.

Ten million children under the age of five die each year, the majority from preventable diseases and malnutrition.

Around 40 million children each year are not registered at birth, depriving them of a nationality and a legal name.

• The above information is an extract from the United Nations High Commission for Refugees' (UNHCR) web site which can be found at www.unhcr.ch Alternatively, see page 41 for their address details.

Back to school

Jonathan Oldham has been looking into how informal educators can support young refugees in schools

There are around 50,000 young refugees aged 18 and under in Britain and the numbers are rising annually. They arrive from around the world, many having experienced conflict and suffered trauma. Young refugees have to adjust to a new culture while also experiencing new hardships, including a language barrier, social isolation, sometimes separation from parents and family, poverty, ill health and discrimination.

Youth workers and other informal educators can play an important role in supporting young refugees, but obviously only if they are in contact with them. It's difficult for young refugees to access mainstream youth provision, but the vast majority do attend school. I decided to look further into how informal educators can support young refugees within school settings. I ran individual and group interviews with young refugees and a range of professionals who work with them.

What came across was that young refugees need support for English language learning and also a range of practical support measures to help them integrate into school life and deal with bullying and racism. There was also a concern to ensure that young refugees are consulted and have a chance to speak out on issues important to them. They would also benefit from a more inclusive curriculum, and the chance to access other services including youth provision.

The people that I spoke to identified a number of areas of work where informal educators could respond to these needs.

Out of school clubs

Out of school clubs help young refugees enjoy a range of informal activities including sports, arts and educational activities and provide vital opportunities for social education.

But they also help meet the other expressed needs: extra language support can be offered by developing reading, writing and communication skills in the clubs. The clubs also help with integration into school life, offering an open and safe environment to come together, where young refugees are not seen as outsiders and can share common experiences.

Peer initiatives

Informal educators can also support schools by developing peer initiatives that involve the young people of the school. Peer reading schemes where young refugees are paired with someone from the same language were a successful way of improving English language. Developing peer anti-bullying projects is another effective way of supporting young refugees and many informal educators have experience of developing these types of projects.

Training and awareness raising

Many people felt that much of the national curriculum was inappropriate for young refugees. Informal educators can help tackle this by supporting schools to explore a more global and inclusive curriculum, including training and awareness sessions to support teachers. In the wider school a more inclusive curriculum can be developed by involving schools in campaigns, exploring issues of rights, celebrating refugee week and other such events and looking at multicultural history and migration of people. These issues can be introduced into PSHE, the new citizenship time and subjects such as geography, history and politics.

Listening to young refugees

Children and young people are often not consulted and listened to. There is a particular need to consult with young refugees and respond positively to their needs – this is their right under Article 12 of the UN Convention on the Rights of the Child. Youth work experience with participatory approaches can be important in helping young refugees to express their views and gain the skills needed to participate in decisions that affect them.

Tackling oppressions

Informed educators should encourage and support schools to tackle racism,

bullying and discrimination by teachers, other workers in the school and young people. The development and enforcement of effective policies for dealing with these issues is particularly important.

Good partnerships

We all know there can be difficulties for youth workers within schools stemming from a clash of cultures. To overcome these differences, common aims should be established from the beginning. This requires informal educators and teachers of all levels to develop strong relationships, based on good communications (including written partnership agreements) and improved resources to fund joint initiatives. Connexions provides us with a good example of a multi-agency partnership model from which to work.

Joint training and awareness sessions will help establish clarity of roles and common ground regarding the aims of the work.

Individual workers can play an active role in developing all of the above initiatives but there also needs

to be support from key organisations. Clearly the youth service with its long history of working with marginalised groups and challenging oppressions is well placed to take a significant role and needs to continue to develop working links with schools.

Workers from NGOs have expertise in refugee issues and working with young refugees, but only a small amount of their work takes place in schools. There is scope for them to improve their links and help cascade their knowledge and expertise.

Youth workers from within refugee communities will generally have a more in-depth understanding of the situation facing young refugees and can offer another level of support. They need to be involved in mainstream youth provision, including schools, and training institutions (particularly those in London where most young refugees are located) need to proactively encourage refugee youth workers to take part in mainstream youth work courses. Goldsmiths College also runs a course

specifically for refugee youth workers and so offers a good practice model to work from.

• The above information is an extract from *Young People Now* produced by the National Youth Agency (NYA). *Young People Now* is the leading monthly magazine for everyone working with young people. Every month it offers news, listings, reviews and in-depth features on issues of concern and special interest. There are also regular pages on health and activity, global issues, politics and power and briefings from the NYA's database youthinformation.com. *Young People Now* is essential reading for youth workers, those in the Connexions Service, health advisers, PSHE teachers and others working in informal education with young people. Published monthly – 12 issues. Annual subscription £22.80 – single copies £2.00 – discounts for bulk orders available on request. Visit their web site at www.nya.org.uk Jonathan Oldham works at Westminster Volunteer Bureau.

Absent friends

An alarming number of refugee children are being denied the chance to go to school – and to integrate

For a year, 14-year-old Kosovan refugee Endrit Shuli tried to go to school in London but was told that there were no places. And so he spent month after month just killing time.

He had had to leave Kosovo because of the war, and came over here without his family. Fleeing a situation of violent conflict, being separated from your family and arriving in an unfamiliar place are a lot for any 14-year-old to deal with, and Endrit yearned to go to school so that he could integrate into British society, learn the language, make some friends and continue with the studies he had assiduously pursued in Kosovo.

'I was forced to leave Kosovo because of the war. I had no choice. I escaped from a terrible situation

By Diane Taylor

and when I first arrived here 17 months ago it was enough for me just to feel safe,' he says. 'But after a while I got bored just watching TV all day in my foster placement. I wanted to make some friends and get on with my education. I wrote to my

MP to ask why there was no school place for me and he wrote back with various excuses. If it was his children who were being deprived of their education, what would he do?'

Endrit is one of thousands of asylum seeker and refugee children who arrive in England expecting to go to school and then find they have to wait months, and in some cases more than a year, before they can get into the classroom. Officials at the Department for Education and Skills say they don't know exactly how many of these children are trying to get a school place because the department does not request that information from local education authorities. In fact the DfES is quick to distance itself from responsibility for this group of children, who for the most part are eager to learn and highly motivated but can't get a seat behind a desk.

While a spokeswoman points out that there is a legal obligation to provide schooling for all children of compulsory school age, irrespective of their immigration status or residence rights, it is for LEAs to make sure they estimate accurately the number of pupils they require funding for on a year-by-year basis.

'LEAs must prepare an annual school organisation plan covering a five-year rolling period. This sets out how the LEA proposes to deal with deficits and surpluses of school provision,' says the DfES spokeswoman. 'LEAs may need to consider temporary expansion of school places from time to time to provide places for refugee and asylum seeker children, perhaps through the provision of temporary classrooms.'

Tina Hyder, programme manager of Save the Children's London development team, which provides support to refugee children, believes that better organisation is required at LEA level to prevent such a large surplus of education-hungry children being unable to get past the school gates.

'Some schools do go out of their way to welcome asylum seekers but others just don't want them,' she says. 'This problem comes down to organisation and political will at LEA level and a lack of firmer guidance from the DfES. These children have a right to education and it's our responsibility to achieve that.'

Save the Children produced a damning report in October 2001, *Cold Comfort: young separated refugees in England*, which found that educational and other services for this group were little more than a lottery, often fragmented and sometimes non-existent.

The problem appears to be more acute in certain London boroughs than in the regions, where asylum seekers are dispersed. There is also a funding discrepancy between London and the regions – schools outside London can claim £500 for every asylum seeker pupil twice a year. This money is not available in London and is seen by critics as part of the government's push to move asylum seekers out of the capital.

Children arrive in England expecting to go to school and then find they have to wait months, and in some cases more than a year, before they can get into the classroom

---

In the London borough of Newham, Yesim Deveci, project coordinator at the Trinity Centre, a community centre that provides education and training for local people including asylum seekers, believes a large majority of the 700 primary and secondary school children who can't access school places in the borough are asylum seekers.

'Increasing numbers of children are just turning up here because they can't find a school place,' she says. 'We offer them English classes in the mornings and try to keep the structure as close as possible to school, but it's not school, it's never going to be school and they shouldn't really be here at all: projects like the one here shouldn't need to exist.

'I have found that many of the children really value education but when they can't get into school their lives are so closed and limited. School can provide stability for them. Their attendance and punctuality here are just amazing. They don't want to play games, they want to learn. They're a teacher's dream. Not allowing these children into school is such a waste of their talents.'

A spokeswoman for Newham council admits that the council experienced some delays in finding school places in the older year groups of the secondary sector because of an unexpectedly high number of children new to the borough. Additional provision had been made, she says,

with the support of the borough's community education service and the local FE college, which was used until school places became available.

Abdul Fofanah, 14, became separated from his family during the bloody conflict in Sierra Leone and escaped to England. He has been waiting more than seven months for a school place, but so far has heard nothing.

'I thought that if I stayed in my country I might be shot dead by the age of 18, and that here I would be able to plan my life. But if I don't go to school, I can't plan for the future,' he says.

'I get so bored sitting at home watching TV all day and I try to study maths and English, but it's hard to do that by myself. I can't believe that you can come to a country like England and not be able to get a school place. I had no idea what to expect of England before I arrived, but one thing I did expect was that I'd be able to go to school.'

Joy Stanton, refugee support coordinator for schools in the London borough of Westminster, is also concerned about the number of children without school places. In Westminster, those who do get school places are helped to integrate with a mixture of mainstream lessons and small group tuition from a team of specialist English as an Additional Language teachers.

'Asylum seekers are amongst the most vulnerable groups in society,' she says. 'However, very many are also resourceful, determined and resilient. Given the right support at the right time, refugee pupils often learn at an accelerated rate and go on to achieve well. When lives have been violently disrupted, school plays a vital part in building a new life.'

Endrit is overjoyed that he has at last been granted a school place, something he says he appreciates beyond measure. 'I see children who have school places and just drop out because they don't realise the importance of learning, and think of people like me who want to get into school but for a long time can't. I feel so much safer in England than I did in my country but without education all the doors in your life close.'

Cold comfort

The lottery of care for young separated refugees in England

A new Save the Children study, *Cold Comfort – young separated refugees in England*, launched today, highlights the lottery of service and care provision given to these vulnerable children across the country. The survey, the first of its kind, funded by the Diana, Princess of Wales Memorial Fund, collated the views of 125 young separated asylum-seekers and refugees and 125 professionals who work with them about the key issues affecting their daily lives.

The report highlights a catalogue of chaotic and disturbing experiences in the young people's contact with immigration, social services and education departments. Payments from local authorities to cover vital day-to-day expenditure such as food varied across authorities. Some young people received no allowance at all; some received local authority vouchers – which carry with them all the stigmas and problems of the national voucher scheme; and a few received small cash payments. Many of the 16-17-year-olds interviewed were placed alone in private accommodation with little or no monitoring and support. In some areas social services departments enter into contracts with private companies, often located a considerable distance from the local authority, to take responsibility for care and support provision. Some private providers are proving inadequate in meeting the needs of these young people.

> 'What you get depends on what social services department you are with, things are definitely getting more difficult as I get older'
> Quote from an 18-year-old boy interviewed in *Cold Comfort*.

On top of worries expressed over actual care provision, the young people were concerned about their treatment on reaching the age of 18. At 18 young refugees often face

Save the Children

dispersal and the trauma of being uprooted. Dispersal breaks the network of friends developed by the young people – forcing them to start again from scratch in a new environment.

The young people also stressed the uncertainty created by the continual delays in the asylum process, this was compounded by mistakes and bureaucratic procedures that are neither child friendly nor clearly explained. Provision of interpreters was also inconsistent and includes using interpreters who speak a completely different dialect to the young person.

Kate Stanley, author of *Cold Comfort*, commented, 'After making an often arduous and dangerous journey to a supposed place of sanctuary, young separated refugees continue to face considerable hardship when they reach England. It seems that here in England, their so-called safe haven is little better than a lottery with support and service provision fragmented and sometimes non-existent. The UK has a duty of care to all young separated refugees regardless of their location, the current state of affairs is frankly unacceptable.'

While recognising the difficulties faced by some social services departments, especially those in port authorities where there are high numbers of young separated refugees, the report calls for more joined-up thinking at government and local authority level. Specifically it calls for a standard series of minimum acceptable standards of care and service provision for young separated refugees and the provision of adequate financial resources to statutory authorities to ensure these standards are met.

• The above information is an extract from Save the Children's web site which can be found at www.savethechildren.org.uk The report, *Cold Comfort*, is available on the web site in PDF format. Also, see page 41 for their address details.

© Save the Children

Refugees in Europe: the real story

Information from Amnesty International

Case studies illustrating how EU countries currently treat refugees – a warning to EU member states formulating common rules for dealing with refugees across Europe.

There are many conflicting images of asylum seekers in Europe – most of them negative.

Amnesty International presents a snapshot of the real situation.

Why have they come here? How are they being treated? Where do they end up?

As part of a European-wide information campaign, Amnesty International traces the journeys of asylum seekers who pass through the asylum system in various countries.

If the lowest common denominator prevails in the proposed EU Common Asylum and Immigration Policy, then what follows will be the sad reality for asylum seekers in a future 'harmonised' Europe.

Why refugees flee

People fleeing violence, torture or other forms of persecution have few options. These 'asylum seekers' are fathers, daughters, sons and mothers.

Afghanistan

'First they rounded up the people in the streets. They then went from house to house and arrested the men of the families except for the very old men. Nothing could stop them, and they did not spare any of the houses. In one house, the mother of a young man whom the Taleban were taking away held onto him saying she would not allow him to go away without her. The Taleban began to hit the woman brutally with their rifle butts. She died. They took away the son and shot him dead. They were our neighbours. When they arrested the people, they tied their hands behind their back and took them away. They took them to areas behind Bazar Kona and fired at them. They executed a lot of people.'

China

'Yusuf (not his real name), a member of the Uighur ethnic minority in China, was arrested for suspected political activity. He was interrogated in an underground chamber. He was given electric shocks with electro-shock batons. The shocks were applied all over his body, including in his mouth and on his penis, causing intense pain. The interrogators hit him on the bones of the legs with a wooden baton. They made him kneel down and hit him on the thighs and the shoulders with the baton. While tortured, he was made to wear a kind of metal helmet which came down over his eyes. The interrogators used this helmet to prevent fatalities; some prisoners, unable to bear the pain of torture, would try and kill themselves by bashing their heads against the walls.'

Angola

'During the attack, the assailants had shot through the locked door of the house of a 27-year-old primary school teacher, Mukwata Kolinus Faniso, then entered the house firing. They killed the teacher and badly injured his wife. Jan Kavura Thikoko, aged over 70, emerged from his house to see what was happening. The attackers reportedly asked his name and, after he replied, shot him dead at point-blank range. In a nearby homestead, another elderly man,

---

Asylum seekers are NOT convicted criminals but in some parts of the European Union, that is how they are being treated

---

Kushamura Kapinga, was also killed and another teacher narrowly escaped detection and possible death because his wife hid him in the bedding. After the attack the villagers abandoned their homes and went to live in the bush some distance to the south where attacks were less likely but where living conditions were precarious.'

Warning: Deficiences in EU policies on third countries, such as inadequate controls of small arms exports from and through EU member states to third countries, may contribute to the conditions which force people to flee their countries and seek refuge in the European Union.

Don't let them off the boat!

Asylum seekers cannot lodge effective claims or tell their story if they are not allowed to 'get off the boat'. This is the case of a Senegalese asylum seeker who was deliberately stopped from landing on EU territory, or communicating with human rights organisations in violation of the international obligations of EU countries.

Seik (not his real name) fled persecution in Senegal. When he arrived by boat in Spain, Spanish police initially prevented him from accessing human rights organisations, which prevented him from lodging an asylum claim.

Seik suffered torture and ill-treatment in Senegal where he was forcibly recruited in 1995 by the guerrilla movement MFDC (who had killed his uncle), and then subsequently captured by the Senegalese military. He managed to flee to Guinea Bissau and then Dakar where he stowed away on the ship *Atlas Rex* which arrived at Vigo harbour in Spain, on 13 November 1995.

Spanish police prevented Seik from coming ashore. Representatives of Amnesty International, other human rights organisations and trade unions were prevented by the police from boarding the ship to speak to him. Despite a court order to allow access to the human rights representatives, Spanish police prolonged the affair by insisting that the shipping company concerned be approached first, by which time the ship had sailed on to the Spanish port of Marin. There, Spanish police once again prevented access to the ship, in breach of the previous judicial decision. Finally, the human rights organisations lodged an asylum application on behalf of Seik and as a result of it, police finally allowed him into the custody of the Red Cross.

Seik's asylum claim was declared inadmissible on 17 November on the grounds that it did not contain the reasons for his claim (due to the fact that he was unable to state these clearly because of lack of access to human rights organisations and interpreters). Despite the fact that the decision acknowledged the difficulties created by the police to access legal assistance and interpreters, as well as the appeals made by Amnesty International to the UNHCR and to the asylum authorities on behalf of Seik, his first appeal was rejected.

On 22 November, Seik was taken to Madrid, for deportation to Dakar. His lawyer then lodged a judicial appeal. On 24 November 1995, the judicial authority allowed Seik to stay in Spain while it examined the claim. Several months later, it declared his claim admissible, forcing the asylum authorities to examine the application on the merits. Months later, tired of waiting for a decision on his asylum claim, Seik decided to obtain a temporary residence permit.

Warning: Some EU countries are already flouting existing international standards concerning the right of access to EU territory for those fleeing persecution. The EU is now in the process of drawing up common immigration rules which do not take into account the international obligations of EU countries towards refugees. Carrier

sanctions, visa regimes, 'reception in the region' schemes designed to control illegal immigration may have dire consequences for refugees fleeing torture, persecution and life-threatening events.

'Safe' countries not so safe

Asylum seekers are not receiving the same level of protection throughout the EU, but they are still returned to the first 'safe' country where they landed, even if this 'safe' country offers them little protection.

Kumar (not his real name), a Sri Lankan, is a typical victim of the varying standards of refugee protection currently operating across the European Union. He has been persecuted by both sides in the independence conflict in Sri Lanka, persecution which was not recognized by at least one EU country – Germany.

Kumar lived in Jaffna in an area controlled by the Tamil organisation, the LTTE, which is engaged in an armed struggle for independence. He was held prisoner by the LTTE for three months and forced to carry out menial work for them.

He escaped to Colombo where he was subsequently arrested by the Sri Lankan army and accused of being a member of the LTTE. He was imprisoned, tortured and ill-treated by the Sri Lankan soldiers. The abuse included being whipped with an electric cable, and strung up by his feet with chains from a bar in the ceiling. While he was hanging, he was beaten on the soles of his feet and lower back with a plastic pipe filled with cement.

After his family paid a bribe to the army, he was released, but subsequently picked up by the army and the police on two further occasions where he was beaten again, including having a heated iron rod pressed against his arm. After his release, he fled to Germany.

Kumar's asylum claim was rejected in Germany after a short, oral hearing, where the courts found that his alleged torture was not relevant to his claim, as these 'excesses of isolated executive organs' could not be imputed to the Sri Lankan state. In addition, as the LTTE was not a 'state', then ill-treatment by this group did not fit into the definition of political persecution by a 'state' and could therefore not be presented as evidence of the need for asylum. He was told to return to Sri Lanka.

Kumar then travelled to the United Kingdom where he again claimed asylum. Despite new medical and other evidence presented in the UK, and the fact that this country grants protection to individuals in the same situation as Kumar, the UK decided to return him to Germany. Under the so-called 'Dublin Convention', he can be returned to the first country where he claimed asylum within the EU because all EU countries are deemed to be 'safe' countries. He argues that Germany did not provide the protection he so desperately needed and fears that from Germany he will be returned to Sri Lanka.

Warning: Even if refugees reach EU territory, their access to fair procedures to determine their asylum claim may be denied in some EU countries. The use of 'safe country' concepts does not ensure that a country is indeed 'safe' or that it will provide effective and durable protection.

Treated like criminals

Asylum seekers are NOT convicted criminals but in some parts of the European Union, that is how they are being treated.

Cardiff Prison, UK: 'The situation in Cardiff prison hit the press when asylum seekers were taken in handcuffs to a local hospital. That shocked many people in Cardiff and elsewhere. When we visited the prison, the authorities told us that asylum seekers were treated the same as other prisoners because they were in a prison regime. In one cell, we met a Pakistani – a very cultured man – who was a scholar, and the author of 37 books. He could not understand why he was being detained. We met a Tamil from Sri Lanka, who had left Sri Lanka because of the daily violence there. He had owned his own bakery. We met an Iranian who was a technician in an oil refinery. We met a man from Kosovo, whose father and brother had disappeared. He was frightened for his life so he decided to flee.'

CD 3527 24DEC01 K.
House of Parliament, 11 July 2001.

Extract from joint letter by asylum seekers quoted by Ann Clwyd MP, 11 July, 2001: 'Here at Cardiff prison we are treated like animals as compared to criminal remand prisoners and those serving sentences. Some of us have never been arrested before, and just found ourselves in a prison cell sharing facilities with convicts of different crimes, people committing suicide and unwarranted bullying from prison officers. You try and seek explanation from the local immigration officer, why you are in prison, "the answer lies with immigration in London" (is) all he is instructed – to help you go back to your country if you are fed up . . . '

Warning: Detention policies and practices in the EU sometimes fail to follow international standards. Not only are asylum seekers held in prisons and prison-like conditions, they are also confined with convicted criminals, yet those seeking asylum have not been convicted of any crime. Detained refugees may suffer the psychological torment of not knowing for how long they will be held and the fear that they may be sent back to their persecutors. Torture victims in particular may suffer further trauma through the psychological stress of detention. Amnesty International believes that detention of asylum seekers should be avoided. No asylum seeker should be detained unless it has been established that detention is necessary, is lawful and complies with one of the grounds recognised as legitimate by international standards. Amnesty International opposes the practice of detaining asylum seekers when adequate and effective safeguards do not exist or are not followed.

• The above information is an extract from *The Asylum Crisis: A Human Rights Challenge for the EU*, produced by Amnesty International in September 2001. For more information see their web site at www.amnesty-eu.org

© *Amnesty International*

The global fallout

Information from the United Nations High Commission for Refugees (UNHCR)

The world will never be the same again following the events of September 11, 2001, in the United States.

This is true, not only for the immediate victims, their families and governments directly involved in the terrorist incidents, but for millions of people who were already among the most vulnerable in the world – refugees and asylum seekers in every part of the globe and virtually the entire population of Afghanistan.

The latest crisis in that country was triggered and perpetuated by the outside world – first when the Soviet army invaded the country, and then when the international community increasingly ignored the sad state in which it was left when foreign soldiers withdrew.

A years-long drought added to the misery and was already ravaging the land when hundreds of thousands of additional civilians became 'collateral damage ' in the latest round of bombings and fighting – some of them dying, others fleeing to 'safer' villages and camps and some escaping across officially closed borders to neighbouring countries.

There has been a remarkable turnaround in military fortunes on the battlefield, but it is not immediately clear what effect that will have on the country's reeling civilian population, especially as another shuddering winter closed in on the region and much of the country was in a virtual state of lawlessness.

Away from Afghanistan, countries rushed to introduce anti-terrorist legislation, beefed up their frontier security and warily eyed foreigners of a 'certain hue'. UNHCR sympathised with legitimate security concerns. But the refugee agency – along with many legislators – was equally worried that any 'rush to legislation' could compromise hard-won legal protections for people with few other defences and could help spread xenophobia already bubbling beneath the surface in some countries against 'bogus 'refugees.

High Commissioner Ruud Lubbers said repeatedly that the 1951 Refugee Convention already offers safeguards to prevent terrorists from infiltrating the international asylum system and noted that refugees were normally the victims of terrorism and not the perpetrators of it.

'Asylum seekers make a perfect target for people who want to invoke old prejudices against foreigners,' Lubbers said. 'Asylum seekers can't answer back.' But could there be a silver lining at the end of this particular crisis? The suffering will continue for some time to come, but with a large slice of luck and renewed commitment to humanitarian principles, just possibly.

Perhaps publics at large, focused for a moment on the crisis, will look behind the scare headlines and discover who refugees are – people just like you and me – and perhaps this time around the industrialised world will not walk away from Afghanistan in its greatest hour of need.

• The above information is an extract from *Refugees* magazine, produced by the UNHCR.

© *UNHCR*

550 illegal immigrants try to storm Channel tunnel

By David Sapsted

The French government faced fresh demands last night for the closure of a refugee centre near Calais after 550 illegal immigrants tried to invade the Channel tunnel in an attempt to reach Britain.

Almost 130 of the first group of 150 would-be asylum seekers got seven miles into the tunnel late on Christmas Day before being turned back by French police.

More than 60 Kent police officers with dogs had raced to the international border in mid-Channel ready to repel the immigrants.

Within hours of the first group breaking through security at the Eurotunnel terminal at Coquelles, near Calais, another wave of 400 arrived and tried to reach the tracks. This time, they were dispersed by French riot police, who fired tear gas and made 50 arrests.

Train services through the tunnel were halted for more than 10 hours, stranding hundreds of holidaymakers, before resuming shortly before 7am yesterday.

All the illegal immigrants were returned to the refugee centre at Sangatte, little more than a mile from the French terminal, where at least 1,400 foreigners currently reside.

Eurotunnel, which has spent more than £5 million strengthening security at Coquelles, yesterday renewed its demand for Sangatte to be closed.

'It is about time the British and French governments sat down and sorted this problem out,' said Kevin Charles, a spokesman.

> **All the illegal immigrants were returned to the refugee centre at Sangatte, little more than a mile from the French terminal, where at least 1,400 foreigners currently reside**

'Eurotunnel has warned about this for 18 months but there are still 1,400 asylum seekers living at Sangatte who are free to come and go as they please. We want something done about Sangatte as quickly as possible.'

Mr Charles added: 'This was a well-planned attempt. It shows that the asylum seekers are increasingly frustrated because they can't get through by other means.

'It appears they deliberately chose Christmas because there are fewer trains – just two an hour – operating.'

David Blunkett, the Home Secretary, held discussions with his French counterpart over the problem in September – a month after 44 Iraqis were rounded up after walking several miles through the tunnel.

But both sides remain sceptical that closing Sangatte would solve the problem of illegal immigrants converging on Calais.

'This is a matter for the French authorities,' said a Home Office spokesman yesterday. 'None of those who got into the tunnel set foot on British soil.'

Although the French are making efforts to tighten security on their side of the Channel, they say Britain's liberal treatment of immigrants makes the country an irresistible magnet.

Services through the tunnel were stopped shortly after 8pm on Christmas Day when the first group of 150 asylum seekers from various

eastern European and Asian countries stormed the terminal, using blankets to smash down an electrified fence and overwhelming the 20 security staff and police on duty.

A few were detained but 129 reached the tunnel and got seven miles inside it before French police rounded them up. They were questioned for three hours and then returned to the Sangatte centre without charge.

By this time, another 400 illegal immigrants had attempted to storm the terminal. French riot police drove back the mob at the main entrance, detaining 50 but allowing the others to return to the refugee centre.

A Calais police spokesman said: 'They have not been charged. The tunnel was shut for several hours while the search was carried out but it is now running normally. There is no problem any more.'

During the tunnel closure, 80 cars and four coaches were forced to delay journeys from Britain to France, as were 30 cars and one coach in Calais heading to Britain.

Eurostar services, which did not operate on Christmas Day, were not affected.

David Hobbs, 29, of London, was heading off on a skiing trip yesterday. He said: 'There are severe delays and we don't know what is happening. We've been waiting here for several hours.'

Vulnerable given a cold welcome to Britain

Charity lifeline for refugees who survive in hostile surroundings on £36 a week

On the final evening, a brick came through her kitchen and landed on the table. By dark there were four locals prowling with two dogs at the back of the house. At 10.30 a voice started screaming through her letterbox in a language she did not understand. 'My boy, who's five, was in the kitchen when the man started shouting. He went hysterical.'

Samira, a Somali refugee, called the police. She says they took two hours to come while she hid with the children in the bedroom. Due to give birth in 10 days, she spoke no English. Welcome to the Beaumont Leys estate, Leicester.

Samira has no idea why the Home Office thought that Leicester was a good place for her to be housed. She knew no one there and was not asked.

When she arrived, a young man with two dogs who lived across the road began watching her come and go, heavily pregnant. He would let the dogs off the lead as she passed with her young children, aged four and three.

He pushed a ball up his jumper to imitate her pregnancy. Then 'Fuck off back to India' appeared in white paint on her window. She is Somalian, with the pale skin of the Barawa tribe. After the brick on her

By Maggie O'Kane

kitchen table, Refugee Action helped her to move.

In October, the charity says, there were 112 reports of racial abuse against refugees in Britain. Under the latest dispersal law implemented this year, refugees are moved around the UK and not allowed to stay in the south-east.

Refugee Action agrees with the dispersal policy in principle, but a lack of preparation means that the most vulnerable of the new arrivals are wandering Britain's towns looking for basics, like doctors and schools.

The Home Office often leaves the job of helping them find their feet to private landlords, who are not always sympathetic. One landlord who provided full board to refugees told them there was not enough food

At 10.30 a voice started screaming through her letterbox in a language she did not understand.

and offered pork sausages and non-halal meat.

Another landlord told Refugee Action: 'They [asylum seekers] have a very loose attitude. If I was them, I would be grateful for what they've got – freshly cooked meals, not necessarily what they want. I don't give a shit where they are from or what they look like. You help us and I'll help you.'

Meanwhile, often-traumatised refugees survive on food vouchers worth £26.54, plus £10 in cash each week.

In Liverpool, which now houses the fourth-largest number of refugees, racists are distributing letters door to door on false notepaper, claiming to be from Liverpool city council. The letters, now being investigated by the police, purport to inform local families that they have been selected for the compulsory housing of a refugee family in their spare bedroom: 'We have allocated the Gandhi family for you to stay with you . . . Payments of £21.50 per month for their keep will be made to you.'

'This type of letter unfortunately surfaces again and again,' says a Liverpool city councillor, Richard Kemp. 'Anyone unlucky enough to receive one should treat it with the contempt it deserves and put it straight in the bin.'

The latest, distributed last month, reads: 'You will be sent an hour-long video to encourage the Breznics in British habits and ways. This will help them to get used to a toilet instead of defecating on newspaper and disposing of it weekly.'

Sandy Buchan, the chief executive of Refugee Action, has been in the refugee business for 20 years, since working with the Vietnamese boat people. He blames much of the racism against refugees on politicians, and some of the tabloid press.

'They talk the language of bogus asylum seekers and spongers – the reality is, who is going to leave their home, their family, their friends and travel across the world to live on £26.54 worth of food vouchers unless they are desperate?

'I've talked to thousands of refugees and passionately believe in the courage, energy, skills and hope they bring to Britain. In the past 10 years I've seen the law humiliate and exclude them. My favourite poster has always been the one that says "Einstein was a refugee".'

Another refugee, Aferodite, crossed the Adriatic sea in an Albanian mafia speedboat, run by the Scafisti, known for dumping their human cargo – often people from inland countries, who cannot swim – into the sea if the Italian police give chase. 'Whatever happens, you don't get the boat confiscated,' a 23-year-old Scafisti told the *Guardian* earlier this year.

Aferodite gave her three children, aged four, two, and nine months, sleeping tablets when warned by the Scafisti that if 'those kids make a noise, they are going in the sea'.

'The worst moment was putting plastic bin bags over the children to keep the waves from them as we were crossing,' she said.

'The waves were huge and we were all wet. It took a couple of hours because they kept switching off the engine in case the Italian police heard the boats.' From Italy they travelled by train and lorry to Dover.

'The journey to Dover took 19 days and we had no clothes to change, only the ones we wore in the boat. The Scafisti told us to throw all our stuff overboard because the boat would get stuck on the beach. I hid my handbag. In it I had my photographs, some food for the children and a dummy for the baby. When the police opened the back of the lorry in Dover I told my children, you are in the land of God.'

Since Aferodite and her three children were dispersed to Liverpool six months ago she keeps the curtains on her windows closed day and night.

'I've talked to thousands of refugees and passionately believe in the courage, energy, skills and hope they bring to Britain. In the past 10 years I've seen the law humiliate and exclude them'

Her tormentors are teenage boys who have defecated on her doorstep and tried to set fire to her back door using old bin bags.

Aferodite arrived in Liverpool to a house furnished with three plates and two mugs. Her landlord disappeared and she called the police to ask where she could find the post office. The local churches helped with furniture.

Since her arrival in April, teenagers stuff rubbish through the letterbox to pile up in the hall. She is frightened they will set it alight when she and her children are sleeping. 'We want to move. We are desperate to move,' she says.

Ngzuzi Kabonga and his family have been moved. He pulls up his stomach and shows the blade mark left by a Congolese soldier who didn't take kindly to the storekeeper who sold wellington boots to the rebels. The sight in his right eye was taken by the same blade.

When the Kabonga family moved to their first house in Liverpool, stones that rattled on his children's bedroom window were not so bad. But in January panes shattered, cutting his youngest child's face. In April it was a brick through the living room window.

Ngzuzi Kabonga is philosophical. Of the Liverpool man coming out of a bookie's who told him to 'get back to Africa you black bastard', Ngzuzi says: 'Maybe he lost money on the horses. Anyway, the son of the man next door speaks to us.'

But for Sandy Buchan of Refugee Action, the racial abuse is not just coming from bad-tempered drunks; it has become institutionalised.

'The political thinking now in this country is that traumatised people must be made to suffer for their sanctuary and "genuine" refugees won't mind,' he says.

'Well they do mind being humiliated and frightened. At least when we lock up criminals we give them a lawyer.'

Women refugees

Britain's asylum system often fails to protect women who are seeking safety from human rights abuses and persecution

Legal protection

One of the difficulties for women fleeing human rights violations has been that the 1951 Refugee Convention envisaged protection for those who had a 'well-founded fear of being persecuted for reasons of race, religion, nationality, membership of a particular social group or political opinion'. Forms of persecution against women are not explicitly mentioned, and while the above list may have simply been a set of examples, it has functioned in refugee law to restrict the granting of refugee status only to the specified categories.

Rigid interpretations of who is a 'refugee' often ignore the way gender shapes the experience of persecution and exclude women's experiences of persecution. For example, women may not be recognised as refugees where their political protest, activism or resistance has taken different forms from those of men. These may include transgressing social mores, for example refusing to wear a veil in some countries; or activities such as hiding people, passing messages or providing community services, food, clothing and medical care.

Procedural barriers

In addition, the asylum determination process itself throws up barriers to women putting forward their case. Little allowance is made for the difficulties women may face in talking publicly about their experiences, especially where these include humiliating forms of torture such as sexual abuse. There is also an acute shortage of information on the human rights abuses inflicted upon women which could be used to support their cases.

Islam and Shah

Some progress in terms of protection for refugee women was made in 1999. A landmark decision in the House of Lords allowed the appeals of two women from Pakistan who claimed asylum in the UK having fled gender-related violence. Both women had been forced to leave their family home by their husbands and risked being falsely accused of adultery. This would not only entail violence from their husbands, but under Sharia law, they risked flogging or death by stoning following criminal proceedings against them. Though lower courts in the UK had accepted that the women had a well-founded fear of persecution, they had been denied full refugee status as they did not fit into one of the categories specified by the 1951 Refugee Convention.

Though the House of Lords' ruling fails to accept women's forms of resistance as 'political', the Islam and Shah case is a major breakthrough for the protection of women as it interprets the category 'membership of a particular social group' more widely to include women where they face discrimination as a group in society and whom the state fails to protect.

> *There are still many changes which need to be made before women can benefit equitably from protection procedures in the UK*

The judgement is not only important for women fleeing gender-related violence, but it is also welcome as it explicitly states that the new, wider interpretation of 'membership of a particular social group' may also allow lesbians and gay men who face persecution on account of their sexuality to receive protection under the Convention.

Gender guidelines

There are still many changes which need to be made before women can benefit equitably from protection procedures in the UK. Asylum Aid assisted the Refugee Women's Legal Group in the drafting of their *Gender Guidelines for the Determination of Asylum Claims in the UK*. We are pressing for these guidelines to be adopted by the UK government in order to ensure that women asylum-seekers are able to access the protection they need from human rights violations.

• The above information is an extract from Asylum Aid's web site which can be found at www.asylumaid.org.uk Alternatively see page 41 for their address details.

© Asylum Aid

Racism and human rights

Refugees, asylum seekers, migrants and internally displaced persons

Throughout the world, refugees, asylum seekers, migrants and internally displaced persons are the victims of racial discrimination, racist attacks, xenophobia and ethnic intolerance. Racism is both a cause and a product of forced displacement, and an obstacle to its solution. In 2000, some 150 million migrants were living outside their countries of birth. Of these, some 50 million people were forcibly displaced as a result of persecution, conflict, and human rights violations.

Industrialised states have introduced a barrage of restrictive policies and practices over the past decade targeting asylum seekers, refugees, and migrants. Negative and inaccurate portrayals of refugees, asylum seekers, and migrants in the media and the inflammatory, xenophobic rhetoric of politicians and public officials in many Western countries have contributed to a climate of hostility towards these groups. There has been an alarming rise in racist and xenophobic violence against asylum seekers, refugees, and migrants in many industrialised countries.

Even traditionally generous host countries in the developing world, often over-burdened with their own social and economic problems, have become increasingly reluctant to host large refugee populations. Faced with mass influxes of refugees from neighbouring countries, many fleeing racist violence in their own countries, governments have closed their borders or attempted to push refugees back over the border. In some cases, explicitly xenophobic and inflammatory statements by political leaders have resulted in attacks on refugee populations, widespread arrests, detention, and even gang rape of refugee women.

The situation
Racism as a root cause of forcible displacement
- In countries such as Burundi, Burma, Bhutan, Indonesia, Sri Lanka, Turkey, and the former Yugoslavia millions of people have been forced to flee their homes as a result of ethnic violence, racism, racial discrimination, and intolerance. In some cases people flee across borders as refugees, in others they are internally displaced within their own countries.

Racism in host countries
Border closures
- Increasingly, refugees who flee situations of ethnic intolerance and violence are unable to find safe refuge in neighbouring countries. Many countries, such as Pakistan, Tajikistan, Guinea, and Thailand have closed their borders to mass influxes of refugees, pushed people back, and failed to provide safe refuge. At the start of the Kosovo refugee crisis in April 1999, for example, Macedonia closed its border to Kosovar Albanian refugees, arguing that the mass influx of refugees of Albanian ethnic origin could critically destabilise the fragile ethnic balance in the country. Refugees were stranded in appalling conditions at the border between Kosovo and Macedonia for days, until the Macedonian government was persuaded to reopen its border after some Western countries agreed to airlift refugees out of the country.

There has been an alarming rise in racist and xenophobic violence against asylum seekers, refugees, and migrants in many industrialised countries

---

Fortress Europe
- The smaller numbers of refugees who arrive in the industrialised states of Western Europe, the United States, and Australia face an equally hostile welcome. Over the past decade the harmonisation of EU asylum policies and the emergence of a fortress Europe approach to asylum and immigration have made it increasingly difficult for certain nationalities and ethnic groups to reach Western European countries.

Barriers to entry
- The imposition of strict visa requirements for nationals of common refugee-producing countries, many of which have well-documented human rights problems, such as China, Burma, Sudan, the Democratic Republic of Congo, Sierra Leone, Turkmenistan, and Rwanda make it almost impossible for refugees fleeing these countries to travel legally to the European Union. Refugees from such countries are highly unlikely to be able to obtain visas from the embassy of their country of destination prior to departure, and are thus forced to flee using invalid or forged documents, or with no documents at all.
- The imposition of heavy fines on airlines and other carriers who transport asylum seekers and migrants without valid documentation, stringent pre-departure immigration checks by airline officials to avoid these fines, and the posting of immigration officials from asylum states to assist in pre-departure immigration checks in common refugee-producing countries, such as Turkey, Sri Lanka, Kenya, Ghana, Senegal, India, and Afghanistan, all pose further obstacles to individuals from particular countries to

exercising their fundamental rights to freely leave their country and seek asylum abroad.

Detention of asylum seekers and migrants

- Those asylum seekers and migrants who manage to evade pre-departure border controls face punitive measures on arrival. In countries such as the US and Australia, for example, asylum seekers and migrants arriving without valid documents face immediate, mandatory detention often for periods of months or years. In the US, asylum seekers and migrants are frequently held in penal facilities alongside accused or convicted criminals, with limited access to NGOs and legal advice or assistance. In Greece, undocumented migrants awaiting deportation, including some who had submitted asylum claims, are held in appalling conditions in detention facilities, with severe overcrowding and lack of access to fresh air or exercise, adequate sleeping accommodations, adequate food, or adequate access to medical care.

Human trafficking and smuggling

- The growing barriers to legal entry into EU and other Western countries has meant that asylum seekers and migrants increasingly turn to the services of opportunistic, corrupt, and dangerous human trafficking and smuggling syndicates who are able to circumvent routine migration controls, often with great risk to their life, liberty, and freedom.

Xenophobia and racism in the public domain

- Restrictive immigration policies are implemented within a climate of hostility and xenophobia towards refugees, asylum seekers, and migrants. Politicians and the media have shamelessly manipulated xenophobic and racist fears in order to muster short-term political support. Politicians, the media, and the general public have portrayed asylum seekers as

bogus and criminals because of the 'illegal' way in which they are forced to enter Western countries. Refugees and migrants are generally blamed for the social and economic ills of society, including rising crime and unemployment. All of these trends have contributed to the alarming rise in racist violence and xenophobia against refugees, asylum seekers, and migrants, particularly throughout Europe, sometimes with the complicit involvement, or tacit approval, of law enforcement agents, and usually without effective sanctions against the perpetrators.

Racism as an obstacle to solving refugee crises

- Racism and ethnic intolerance continue to prevent refugees from exercising their right to return to their countries or places of origin. Some 100,000 refugees from Bhutan, over one million refugees and displaced persons from the former Yugoslavia, an estimated 6 million Palestinian refugees, and some 30,000 black Mauritanians have all been obstructed from returning to their

countries or place of origin on grounds of their race, religion, ethnicity, or nationality.

Disparity in the international response

- There is gross regional disparity in the international response to refugee crises. The Kosovo refugee crisis, one of the largest and most high profile refugee crises in Europe since the Second World War, generated an outpouring of international support and assistance. This has not been matched in refugee situations in other parts of the world, namely Africa, Asia, and the Middle East. Large, long-term refugee populations in countries such as Pakistan with some two million Afghan refugees, Iran with 1.5 million Afghan refugees, Guinea with 400,000 Sierra Leonean and Liberian refugees, and Tanzania with over half a million refugees from the Great Lakes region, have been sorely neglected by the international community. The lack of international assistance to these refugee situations has resulted in diminishing protection, poor living conditions,

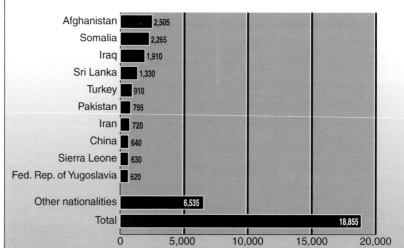

Top ten applicant nationalities – Q3 2001

Afghanistan	2,505
Somalia	2,265
Iraq	1,910
Sri Lanka	1,330
Turkey	910
Pakistan	795
Iran	720
China	640
Sierra Leone	630
Fed. Rep. of Yugoslavia	620
Other nationalities	6,535
Total	18,855

- The number of applications from Afghan nationals remained at the same level as Q2, and was the highest applicant nationality for the second consecutive quarter.

- Applications from Somali nationals rose by 60% in this quarter – a third more than in Q3 2000.

- The number of Iraqi applications rose by 78% from 1,075 in Q2, though is only 1% higher than in Q1, and a quarter less than Q3 2000.

- The top 10 nationalities accounted for 65% of all applications, and the top 3 for 35%

Source: Home Office, Crown Copyright

and an increasing unwillingness by host states to take in new influxes of refugees.

Key recommendations

- States should recognise that discrimination against refugees, asylum seekers, migrants, and internally displaced persons is a contemporary form of racism. Governments and regional bodies should take steps to reverse policies and practices that discriminate against refugees, asylum seekers, and migrants; reinforce the existing international refugee protection regime; and introduce new protection standards where necessary.

- All states should ratify and fully implement the 1951 Convention Relating to the Status of Refugees and the 1967 Protocol and ensure that these instruments are applied to all asylum seekers and refugees without discrimination. Those states that have maintained a geographical limitation incompatible with the non-discriminatory intention of the 1967 Protocol should withdraw it.

- The fundamental principles of non-refoulement and non-discrimination enshrined in these international instruments should be scrupulously observed. In particular governments should not return asylum seekers to so-called 'safe third countries' where they may be at risk of direct or indirect refoulement, or other serious human rights violations. States should immediately cease the discriminatory practice of excluding asylum seekers on the basis of their country of origin without a serious consideration of their asylum claim. Such practices could result in returning refugees to countries where they may face persecution, torture, and even death.

- States should ratify the 1990 International Convention on the Protection of the Rights of All Migrant Workers and Members of Their Families.

- States should ensure that they respond urgently, effectively, and without discrimination to situations of mass displacement and humanitarian crises regardless of geographical proximity or political interests. States should take urgent action to address the needs of the 25 to 30 million internally displaced persons worldwide. In particular, states should apply the Guiding Principles on Internal Displacement, particularly those provisions relating to non-discrimination.

- States should take immediate steps to reverse asylum and immigration policies and directives that discriminate on the basis of race, nationality, and ethnicity. In particular, policies such as visa requirements for nationals of common refugee-producing countries, carrier sanctions, the posting of immigration officials in countries of origin, pre-departure immigration checks, and mandatory detention policies should be scrupulously evaluated to ensure that they do not discriminate on the grounds of race, nationality or ethnicity.

- States should ensure that they respond effectively to and fully investigate all incidents of racial and related violence against migrants, asylum seekers and refugees; that they provide compensation and redress to the victims; and take active measures to arrest and prosecute the perpetrators.

- Governments and public officials should avoid the direct or indirect use of language that may contribute to a hostile environment within which racism, xenophobia and related intolerance against refugees, asylum seekers and migrants flourish and acts of racist violence are rationalised; they should counteract inaccurate, racist and xenophobic stereotypes of refugees, asylum seekers and migrants in the media; and encourage informed public debate on asylum and immigration matters.

- The above information is an extract from Human Rights Watch's web site which can be found at www.hrw.org

Most asylum seekers are smuggled into Britain

Seven out of 10 asylum seekers entering Britain were helped by an agent or smuggler, a study has found.

Dr Andrew Bateman, a researcher from the University of Wales in Swansea, analysed the cases of 371 asylum seekers and found that 72 per cent used smuggler gangs and only five per cent used family contacts.

The asylum seekers came from 46 countries, dominated by Iraq (12 per cent of the sample), Kosovo (15 per cent) and Somalia (23 per cent), he told the conference.

He said that around 70 per cent of the 98,000 refugees who entered Britain in the year 2000 used smugglers, paying them up to £10,000.

A typical journey might involve a flight to Dubai, then to Moscow, from where the refugees would enter Europe.

Asylum seekers can be detained, judges rule

The home secretary, David Blunkett, yesterday won his appeal against a high court ruling which could have led to the release from detention of hundreds of asylum seekers and compensation running into millions of pounds for wrongful imprisonment.

The appeal court ruled that it has been legal for the home secretary to detain for up to 10 days more than 8,000 asylum seekers at Oakington detention centre in Cambridgeshire since it opened in March last year while their 'fast-track' claims were decided.

Three appeal court judges, including the master of the rolls, Lord Phillips, said in their ruling that such a short of period of detention was justified especially when the government was faced with 7,000 new asylum applications every month even though detention in such circumstances might go beyond what the European court of human rights might require.

'No responsible government can simply shrug its shoulders and do nothing. A short period of detention is not an unreasonable price to pay in order to ensure the speedy resolution of the claims of a substantial proportion of this influx. In the circumstances such detention can properly be described as a measure of last resort,' the judges said in their ruling.

However, the appeal court did stress that the use of such detention for 'a significant length of time' would be objectionable to 'most right thinking people'.

The original ruling knocked the government's immigration policy off course and so frustrated Mr Blunkett he angrily attacked 'triumphalist' human rights lawyers and warned them not to undermine reforms expected to be announced in the next fortnight.

The home secretary expressed his delight yesterday that the original

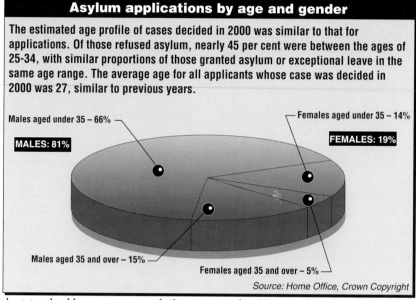

Asylum applications by age and gender

The estimated age profile of cases decided in 2000 was similar to that for applications. Of those refused asylum, nearly 45 per cent were between the ages of 25-34, with similar proportions of those granted asylum or exceptional leave in the same age range. The average age for all applicants whose case was decided in 2000 was 27, similar to previous years.

Males aged under 35 – 66%
MALES: 81%
Females aged under 35 – 14%
FEMALES: 19%
Males aged 35 and over – 15%
Females aged 35 and over – 5%

Source: Home Office, Crown Copyright

decision had been overturned. 'I am extremely pleased that the court has found in favour of the Home Office and that common sense has prevailed. This rational and understandable judgment reinforces confidence in our judicial and legal system. Oakington is an important element in the effective operation of tough but fair immigration controls.'

The government had taken the unusual step of bringing out its biggest guns to fight the case with the attorney general, Lord Goldsmith, present in court.

But the lawyers who represented the four Kurdish asylum seekers at the centre of the original case said the decision was 'very disappointing' and claimed it would greatly extend the home secretary's powers of detention.

Their solicitor, Michael Hanley, said: 'The Home Office does not have to show that detention is necessary to prevent unlawful immigration. If the appeal court is right, this leaves asylum seekers without any significant protection to the right to liberty.

'It gives the Home Office the ability to detain purely for administrative convenience. We will seek to establish this is unlawful in an appeal

to the House of Lords.' Leave was granted for the Lords appeal.

The decision also appears to clear the way for the expansion of the use of such fast-track detention centres, but Home Office sources said yesterday they had no immediate plans to open another Oakington. It is expected though that Mr Blunkett will announce plans in the next fortnight to increase the use of 'open door' reception centres for new asylum seekers.

Louise Pirouet of Oakington Concern, which was set up to monitor conditions at the former RAF barracks, said it was not a prison and should not be used as one. 'Asylum seekers need only be asked to agree to reside at the detention centre and be available for interview. They do not need to be locked up,' she said.

• A human rights litigation unit is to be launched by Liberty member Cherie Booth QC next week to pursue cases under the Human Rights Act. The Liberty unit will be based at Matrix Chambers, central London.

• By Alan Travis, Home Affairs Editor

Asylum seekers and work

Government policies are keeping too many refugees and asylum seekers from working, according to Industrial Society report

Refugees and asylum seekers are being actively hampered from working, through a combination of muddled Government migration policy, employer ignorance and media-backed public prejudice according to a new report, *A Poor Reception, Refugees and asylum seekers: welfare or work?* published today by the Industrial Society.

Among the report's policy recommendations (listed below) key suggestions include ensuring that permission to work after six months should be given automatically other than in exceptional cases. In addition the Government needs to develop a national database of refugee and asylum seekers' skills linked to the Employment Service and other relevant agencies. A national scheme for recognising qualifications needs to be developed along with standardisation of English-language testing to help easily identify the level of language skill of an applicant. Finally the Government needs to change perceptions by running an education initiative designed to shift public opinion and educate employers about the skills and experience of most asylum seekers and refugees.

The report argues that asylum seekers and refugees face unnecessarily high barriers to work. Best estimates indicate that up to 80% of asylum seekers are unemployed despite many having high levels of skills. People with refugee status and individuals granted Exceptional Leave to Remain (ELR) are automatically permitted to work. Asylum seekers in practice have permission to work granted after six months to the principal asylum seeker (though not their families). The report argues that the Government's declared intent of creating employment opportunity for all – full employment – will be unattainable if refugees and asylum seekers continue to be excluded in such large numbers from the labour market.

> **Asylum seekers and refugees face unnecessarily high barriers to work. Best estimates indicate that up to 80% of asylum seekers are unemployed despite many having high levels of skills**

A Poor Reception identifies three areas where barriers to work for refugees and asylum seekers have been erected. First, employers are under- or ill-informed and face the fear of stiff penalties (up to £2000 fine) should they employ an illegal immigrant. There is no standard permission-to-work document issued to refugees and asylum seekers, the wording of immigration papers is ambiguous and unclear and employers have reported that often the immigration authorities have been unhelpful in clarifying an applicant's status.

Second, discriminatory attitudes among the general public towards asylum seekers in particular, have been encouraged by parts of the media who perpetuate the myth that such people are 'work-shy scroungers' despite the fact that immigrants contribute more in taxes and national insurance contributions than they consume.

Third, many new arrivals to the UK lack good English. Those that do have good English (up to NVQ level 4) have far better employment prospects. However as big a problem is the lack of recognition of formal qualifications gained overseas meaning many highly skilled refugees and asylum seekers suffer downward professional mobility.

The report is launched against a background of mass migration

worldwide – more so than at any time since the second world war. Such migration is being driven by a mix of political oppression, armed conflict, the widening gulf between rich and poor countries and the expansion of awareness of other opportunities via mass media and travel. There are currently 13 million people around the world who are either refugees or asylum seekers of which 2.5 million are in Europe and just over 10 per cent of these (265,000) are in the UK.

Overall the report recommends 10 core policy initiatives and reforms.

- Perceptions need to be changed by running a major public education initiative designed to shift public opinion and educate employers about the skills and experience of most asylum seekers and refugees.
- There is a need for clear guidelines on the legal obligations of firms wishing to employ asylum seekers and refugees and easy access to advice and information.
- Partnerships between employers, refugee agencies and organisations working with refugees should be seen as the way forward.
- Migration policy needs to be overhauled and seen as a continuum from entry, to settlement through to integration. A new policy should include all groups of migrants.
- A standard work permit must be issued to all those with permission to work. It could include a help line for employers and could also double as an ID card.
- A National Insurance number should be issued at the same time as permission to work is granted and permission to work should be granted to partners of principal applicants.
- Permission to work after six months should be given automatically other than in exceptional cases.
- A national skills database of refugees and asylum seekers should be established and fed through to Employment Service and other relevant agencies.
- Skills and qualifications assess-

ments of asylum seekers should begin while a decision on status is awaited. This will help speed up the integration process for successful applicants.
- A national scheme for recognising qualifications is needed and English-language testing must be standardised so that employers can easily identify the level of language skill of an applicant.

Asylum seekers and refugees in reality don't fit the popular stereotype as wasters and scroungers. They're young, skilled, willing and keen to work

---

As Gill Sargeant, co-author of the report, says, 'Asylum seekers and refugees in reality don't fit the popular stereotype as wasters and scroungers. They're young, skilled, willing and keen to work. It is a matter of national disgrace that nearly four out of five asylum seekers and refugees are being excluded from British workplaces. They want the work, employers want workers and the Government says it wants employment opportunity for all. It's clearly high time that the Government got its act together on migration policy and made sure that those allowed to live in this country are also allowed to work in this country.'

Notes
Refugees in Britain
- In the year 2000 there were 80,315 applications for asylum in the UK with the top nationalities being Iraq, Iran, Sri Lanka, The Federal Republic of Yugoslavia and Afghanistan
- The average age of applicants was 27 and over 80% of applicants were male.
- Around a third of applications for asylum in 2000 resulted in a grant of asylum or exceptional leave to stay.

Definitions
Asylum seekers
People who have applied for asylum but whose application has not yet been determined by the Home Office.

Exceptional leave to remain (ELR)
A discretionary grant allowing the individual to stay in the UK for a period up to 4 years. After 4 years a person with ELR may apply for indefinite leave to remain.

Refugees
Refugees have been granted refugee status under the terms of the 1951 United Nations Convention. At the same time they are granted indefinite leave to remain, they are entitled to a Convention travel document and the right to a family reunion. They are also permitted to work and hold the same rights as any resident of the United Kingdom.

Economic migrants
Economic migrants are people who leave their home country in search of work and employment. Generally the UK has a restrictive attitude to economic migration. Today entry to the UK is through the work permit system usually only granted to highly skilled professionals or for smaller work-related categories such as students or vacation workers.

- The Industrial Society are the UK's leading thinkers and advisers on the world of work. Everything we do – from consultancy to research, from training to advocacy, from education to advisory services – is driven by our commitment to improve working life. We are a wholly independent, not-for-profit body and hold Royal Charter status. Our members include companies of every size, from every sector of the economy, along with public sector organisations, charities and trade unions.

• The above information is an extract from the Industrial Society's web site which can be found at www.indsoc.co.uk Alternatively, see page 41 for their address details.
© *The Industrial Society 2002*

Asylum seekers and health

A BMA and Medical Foundation for the Care of the Victims of Torture dossier

Asylum seekers are mong the most vulnerable people in Britain. Displaced from their homes, in flight from persecution, often subject to mental and physical violence, they seek sanctuary in countries with more liberal, compassionate reputations. Yet on arrival in the UK their health, already precarious, often deteriorates.[1] And for good reason. The Government's system for the handling of asylum seekers is not focused on helping but on deterring them. Present procedures are not compassionate but punitive.

Health care for asylum seekers in Britain is patchy, belated and often inappropriate. The entitlements are there and certainly there are some excellent initiatives. But entitlement is not the same as access in practice. There are dedicated clinics in Leeds and Folkestone. The Medical Foundation for the Care of the Victims of Torture (Medical Foundation) has years of committed experience. But these are too few and too under-resourced. The UK signed the United Nations Convention Relating to the Status of Refugees in 1951. By doing so it committed itself to providing health care to refugees but it is failing.

What follows is a dossier of cases, passed to the BMA by health care professionals, with their patients' agreement,[2] that documents, again and again, the personal cost of this failure, measured in the suffering of refugees. The BMA and the Medical Foundation urge the Government in its current review of asylum policy, to abolish vouchers and forced dispersal and develop a more humane system.

Case 1

This 18-month-old toddler was referred to the Paediatric Department. The child wasn't crawling. Most children start crawling before the age of one. I am concerned that this child may have cerebral palsy,

muscular dystrophy or an unusual metabolic disorder. Luckily a health advocate is present at the consultation since both the parents speak no English. She tells me that the parents are very distressed about the poor quality of their accommodation. The whole family live in one room. The double bed, which they share, fills the room. It then becomes very apparent why the child has not yet started to crawl. There is simply no space in the home environment to crawl.

Case 2

I saw a baby with a terrible skin condition. His body was covered in sores, which were oozing. The family was constantly uprooted from one hostel to another. Because of this constant upheaval no GP/specialist was looking after him. I prescribed bath oils and creams and arranged for consultant follow-up. I wondered

how the family would be able to care for the baby. There was limited access to hot water in the hostel. I worried that the family would be dispersed before the consultant followed them up. I have no idea what happened to the boy.

Case 3

I have seen some asylum seekers' children who are failing to gain weight. At times it is easy to see why. Asylum seekers are often forced to live in terrible housing. There may be 10 families sharing a living space. Due to the cramped conditions, the children are at more risk of accidents particularly if cooking, feeding, washing and sleeping are all being done in the same room. Outbreaks of diarrhoea and vomiting are more common when people live in crowded conditions. In some cases mums don't have the facilities to sterilise bottles adequately. Parents may also suffer from mental health problems.

Case 4

He was a man with mental health problems and was dispersed to a northern city where he knew no one and had no community support. His mental illness deteriorated. He began to eat poison and was picked up by police as he walked on the motorway on his way back to London.

Case 5

She had come to A and E because she was scared that she might be pregnant. She had fled her country two weeks previously. Soldiers had attacked her home in the middle of the night. She had been multiply raped and fled for her life. She doesn't know what happened to her children. Someone she met on the street, from her community, was letting her sleep on the floor. I arranged the appropriate medical follow-up and referred her to the Medical Foundation.

Case 6

Ms B is a survivor of cruel torture and violence in her home country and is applying for asylum. She recently delivered a baby, her firstborn. She is unable to breastfeed and, as an asylum seeker supported by the National Asylum Support Service, cannot receive milk tokens. Many women in this situation have to water down the milk for their babies, as otherwise they cannot make it last long enough.

Case 7

I saw a young man whose face has been mutilated as a result of torture. He is now blind, speaks no English and lives alone. He is totally isolated in a place where he can't communicate. He is extremely depressed and distressed. Imagine not being able to communicate. In a way it is a continuation of torture.

Case 8

I was asked to do a report on an asylum seeker who had been dispersed. We arranged to meet on a weekday morning. I was astounded to learn that he had set off from his home at 10pm the previous night. He had walked 35 miles throughout the night because he didn't have any money for the bus fare. He has to survive on £10 cash per week.

Case 9

An asylum seeker was forced to flee a regime under which as a doctor he was forced to amputate the noses and ears of army conscripts who had deserted. This doctor is studying for exams that will allow him to work in

this country. He wants to contribute to the society that has given him refuge, not be forced to depend on it.

Case 10

A young man was refused accommodation by the local homeless unit. He ended up sleeping in a car for months. He had severe mental health problems and was at serious risk of self-harm. We were all very worried about him at the practice and asked the local homeless unit to come and explain to us what the problem was – we were told they no longer had a duty to house single people, they have 8,000 people on their lists and 150 properties available. I have had no training in dealing with asylum seekers – it's all been learning on the job.

Case 11

I know of a doctor in this practice who has given money on more than one occasion from her own purse to asylum seekers who were utterly desperate. They often come on a Friday afternoon when social services are closed. They are desperate for money for food, often food to feed their children.

Case 12

A few weeks ago we received a fax from the local Primary Care Group (PCG) informing us that a number of refugees would be arriving in the area, and that we should be prepared to take them on to our lists. Despite this information having been with the PCG for two weeks the first that our practice knew of it was a contact from the practice manager of a neighbouring practice informing us that they had had a number of refugees signing on with them that morning and that we should be prepared to do the same. Although we are a port of entry it is not usual

for us to deal with asylum seekers and refugees and from my experiences in dealing with an asylum seeker previously, I knew that the infrastructure to cater for the special needs of this group is simply not available locally. As a consequence asylum seekers can feel extremely isolated and ignored by the system and it can be a real struggle to get even the most basic of their needs addressed, if at all. There has been no offer of special training for us, or even a contact list for groups who offer support to refugees, which do not seem to exist outside London. Although I am happy to look after these individuals I do not feel adequately prepared to do so. Although the numbers we are talking about are small, the needs of this group are complex and will take up a lot of our time, even assuming that an interpreter is made available. I feel that these people deserve better and am worried that my best may not be good enough.

Although all these case histories are based on real cases, certain key details have been altered to maximise the privacy of the individuals concerned.

• Case histories provided by the following doctors:
Dr Kate Adams, Senior House Officer
Dr James Barratt, consultant psychiatrist
Dr Jackie Bucknall, consultant paediatrician
Dr Angela Burnett
Dr Sheila Cheeroth GP
Dr Sam Everington GP
Dr Peter Le Feuvre GP
Dr Anna Livingstone GP
Dr Kay Saunders GP
Dr Ron Singer GP

References
1   See, for example, A Burnett and M Peel, 'Health Needs of Asylum Seekers and Refugees', BMJ 2001; 322:544-547 (3 March)
2   In cases where it has proved impossible to obtain explicit consent, doctors have provided a general summary drawn from their experience of many similar cases.

© British Medical Association (BMA)
October 2001

Protecting refugees

An introduction

UNHCR was created to provide international protection for refugees and to find durable solutions to their plight. In certain circumstances, UNHCR is also expected to help and protect other groups of people in a refugee-like situation. UNHCR's unique mandate has required it since 1950 to monitor situations that could make people take flight and to take appropriate action when refugees' rights are threatened. Action includes both operational and other types of responses, such as intervening with relevant authorities on behalf of refugees and proposing appropriate remedial action. UNHCR must work in close co-operation with governments, who bear the primary responsibility to protect the human rights of people on their territory.

Securing basic rights

Protecting refugees involves ensuring that their basic human rights are respected in accordance with international standards. To do this, UNHCR works both in refugees' countries of origin and in countries of asylum. The first step towards protecting refugees is often ensuring non-rejection at borders and access to safety. Operations in border areas, camps, airports and detention centres allow staff to monitor and address the protection problems that refugees frequently encounter during their flight and asylum and for some time after their return home. A crucial protection activity is to ensure that asylum-seekers are given access to status determination procedures and, along with refugees, are protected from forced return to a situation of danger. In complex displacement emergencies – typically involving many humanitarian actors as well as increasing numbers of inter-governmental organisations and even the military – UNHCR plays a pivotal co-ordinating role for organisations that share its aims. Its paramount concerns are to secure

the rights to life (and to food, shelter and health care) and liberty.

Ensuring asylum

The fundamental UNHCR protection activity is ensuring that refugees and others in need of international protection are recognised and granted asylum. When national authorities cannot or will not implement procedures to identify refugees, UNHCR's staff are often deployed to thoroughly assess individual cases. Usually, UNHCR helps states to establish adequate refugee status determination procedures through training, advice and provision of background information on the refugees' countries of origin. Another important concern is to ensure that recognised refugees receive documentation attesting to their status to secure appropriate treatment and, in some cases, to avoid the denial or loss of nationality. When host governments fail to guarantee refuge to people in need of protection, UNHCR co-ordinates efforts to ensure their safety and rights. This might be through political approaches to governments, by mobilising other actors in the

---

Protecting refugees involves ensuring that their basic human rights are respected in accordance with international standards

---

national and international arena, or through physical intervention, like transfer to safer locations or resettlement. UNHCR endeavours to see that governments keep not only to the letter but also to the spirit of international refugee law.

Legal and resettlement assistance

Resettlement remains a vital instrument of international protection and a durable solution for a small number of carefully screened refugees who need to be moved for security reasons or because of their vulnerability. Special resettlement programmes are designed to benefit women at risk and other groups with special needs. UNHCR's protection officers usually identify refugees personally for resettlement. In recent years clear and consistent criteria have been rigorously introduced in order to improve this process. Through continuing consultations with governments and agency partners UNHCR develops strategies for meeting resettlement needs in a coherent and transparent manner.

Protection and security risks

In carrying out protection work on the ground UNHCR and partner agency staff increasingly face physical risk. In recent years, forced population displacement has often occurred in situations of armed conflict or violent civil disorder, and the mere presence of UNHCR or other humanitarian staff can arouse hostility. The number of security incidents is rising sharply. Since January 1999, five UNHCR staff members have been killed in the line of duty – four in the month of September 2000 alone.

Promoting refugee law

In addition to their operational protection role, UNHCR's field offices engage in a range of other activities to promote the international refugee protection system. These include promoting accession to the 1951 Convention relating to the Status of Refugees and its 1967 Protocol, to the 1954 Convention relating to the Status of Stateless Persons and to the 1961 Convention on the Reduction of Statelessness. In 1999, UNHCR launched a campaign to promote accession to the 1951 Convention that will culminate on its 50th anniversary in July 2001. Other promotional activities include helping states to enact or revise national refugee legislation, strengthening relevant legal and judicial institutions, training staff of government and non-governmental agencies and liaising with relevant human rights bodies. UNHCR is also involved in: research and advice on new laws and regulations affecting persons of concern to the Office; technical and financial support for law schools and civil service institutes, to develop refugee law courses; and support for human rights and refugee rights advocacy groups, legal aid centres and non-governmental organisations with an interest in refugee protection.

Finding solutions

UNHCR's mandate is to continue to protect refugees until a viable and lasting solution to their predicament has been found. The preferred solution for refugees is generally voluntary repatriation in safety and dignity. When repatriation takes place, UNHCR continues to ensure respect for basic rights during the process of return, and works with returnees for some time after their repatriation, monitoring their treatment and promoting their reintegration. In other cases, however, return under satisfactory conditions remains elusive. Then UNHCR looks into other long-term solutions. These include helping refugees to successfully integrate into the society of their country of asylum or to move to a third country (where they may resettle). In either case, refugees are helped to become self-reliant and, eventually, obtain citizenship.

Protecting other persons of concern

UNHCR's expertise is also often called upon to protect and assist people other than refugees and asylum-seekers.

Returnees

This term applies to people who had been of concern to UNHCR when outside of their country of origin and who remain so after their return, but only for a limited period of time. UNHCR monitors returnees until conditions in the country of origin are considered stable, national protection is again available and returnees have reintegrated in their home communities. UNHCR ensures that amnesties or other guarantees offered by the country of origin are respected and that returnees enjoy the same human rights and fundamental freedoms as their fellow citizens. UNHCR may also help returnees acquire identity documents, obtain access to public institutions and social services and repossess their land and other private property.

Internally displaced persons

UNHCR has increasingly been requested to intervene to protect and assist internally displaced persons (IDPs). Although UNHCR often encounters IDPs by virtue of their being mixed with other categories of person of concern to UNHCR (such as refugees and returnees), UNHCR has on a number of occasions been requested to intervene solely on their behalf. In 2000, UNHCR published guidelines setting out the conditions for its involvement with IDPs. The Office also participates actively in the UN inter-agency task force on IDPs, which is intended to co-ordinate the UN's efforts on behalf of IDPs and to ensure they receive adequate protection and assistance, in accordance with the UN's Guiding Principles on Internal Displacement.

Stateless persons

In carrying out its mandate regarding stateless persons, UNHCR increases awareness of the problem of statelessness and the range of solutions available to eliminate it. The 1954 Convention relating to the Status of Stateless Persons and the 1961 Convention on the Reduction of Statelessness provide a comprehensive framework by which to address current cases of statelessness and avoid like situations in the future. UNHCR provides technical support and advice to states on issues related to statelessness, while encouraging them to accede to the relevant conventions and incorporate their provisions into national law and practice. As part of this effort, UNHCR provides training for government officials and UNHCR staff, participates in government and intergovernmental forums dealing with statelessness, and encourages closer co-operation among states to resolve situations of statelessness.

• The above information is an extract from UNHCR's web site which can be found at www.unhcr.ch
© *United Nations High Commission for Refugees (UNHCR)*

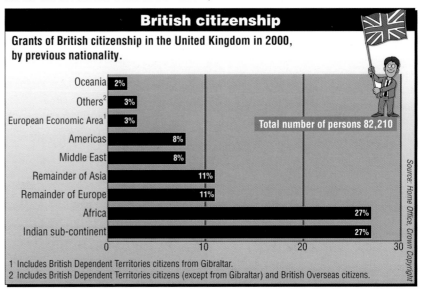

British citizenship

Grants of British citizenship in the United Kingdom in 2000, by previous nationality.

- Oceania 2%
- Others[2] 3%
- European Economic Area[1] 3%
- Americas 8%
- Middle East 8%
- Remainder of Asia 11%
- Remainder of Europe 11%
- Africa 27%
- Indian sub-continent 27%

Total number of persons 82,210

1 Includes British Dependent Territories citizens from Gibraltar.
2 Includes British Dependent Territories citizens (except from Gibraltar) and British Overseas citizens.

Source: Home Office, Crown Copyright

ADDITIONAL RESOURCES

You might like to contact the following organisations for further information. Due to the increasing cost of postage, many organisations cannot respond to enquiries unless they receive a stamped, addressed envelope.

Amnesty International – British Section
99-119 Roseberry Avenue
London, ECR 4RE
Tel: 020 7814 6200
Fax: 020 7 833 1510
E-mail: info@amnesty.org.uk
Web site: Web site:
www.amnesty.org.uk
Amnesty International is a world-wide human rights movement which is independent of any government, political faction, ideology, economic interest or religious creed.

Asylum Aid
28 Commercial Street
London, E1 6LS
Tel: 020 7377 5123
Fax: 020 7247 7789
E-mail: info@asylumaid.org.uk
Web site: www.asylumaid.org.uk
Asylum Aid provides free legal advice and representation to refugees and asylum seekers seeking safety in the UK from persecution.

British Medical Association (BMA)
BMA House, Tavistock Square
London, WC1H 9JP
Tel: 020 7387 4499
Fax: 020 7383 6400
E-mail: enquiries@bma.org.uk
Web site: www.bma.org.uk
Please note that the BMA does not have the resources to deal with individual enquiries. However, they will respond to teachers' enquiries.

CAFOD – The Catholic Agency for Overseas Development
Romero Close, Stockwell Road
London, SW9 9TY
Tel: 020 7733 7900
Fax: 020 7274 9630
E-mail: hqcafod@cafod.org.uk
Web site: www.cafod.org.uk
CAFOD is the development agency of the Catholic Church in England and Wales and works in partnership to tackle the causes of poverty regardless of race, religion or politics.

Children of the Storm
61 Oak Grove
Cricklewood
London, NW2 3LS
Tel: 020 7435 4880
Fax: 020 7435 4880
Web site: www.cotstorm.demon.co.uk
Children of the Storm works to cater for the emotional and material needs of the increasing number of young asylum seekers entering Britain.

Human Rights Watch
33 Islington High Street
London, N1 9LH
Tel: 020 7713 1995
Fax: 020 7713 1800
E-mail: hrwuk@hrw.org
Web site: www.hrw.org
Human Rights Watch is dedicated to protecting the human rights of people around the world.

The Industrial Society
49 Calthorpe Road
Edgbaston
Birmingham, B15 1TH
Tel: 01870 400 1000
Fax: 01780 400 1099
The Industrial Society is an independent, not-for-profit campaigning body with over 10,000 member organisations from every part of the economy.

Oxfam
Oxfam House
274 Banbury Road
Oxford, OX2 7DZ
Tel: 01865 311311
Fax: 01865 312600
E-mail: oxfam@oxfam.org.uk
Web site: www.oxfam.org.uk
Oxfam GB is a development, relief, and campaigning organisation dedicated to finding lasting solutions to poverty and suffering around the world.

Refugee Action (RA)
The Old Fire Station, 3rd Floor
150 Waterloo Road
London, SE1 8SB
Tel: 020 7654 7700
Fax: 020 7401 3699
Web site: www.refugee-action.org
Refugee Action is an independent charity that supports refugees and asylum seekers to build new lives in the UK.

Refugee Council
Bondway House
3 Bondway
London, SW8 1SJ
Tel: 020 7820 3000
Fax: 020 7582 9929
E-mail: info@refugeecouncil.org.uk
Web site: www.refugeecouncil.org.uk
The Refugee Council is the largest organisation in the UK working with asylum seekers and refugees. They believe asylum seekers and refugees should be treated with understanding and respect.

Save the Children
17 Grove Lane
Camberwell
London, SE5 8RD
Tel: 020 7703 5400
Fax: 020 7703 2278
Web site:
www.savethechildren.org.uk and
www.savethechildren.org.uk/
rightonline
www.savethechildren.org.uk/
education
Save the Children is the leading UK charity working to create a better world for children. Works in 70 countries helping children in the world's most impoverished communities.

United Nations High Commission for Refugees (UNHCR)
21st Floor, Millbank Tower
21-24 Millbank
London, SW1P 4QP
Tel: 020 7828 9191
Fax: 020 7222 4813
Web site: www.unhcr.ch
UNHCR promotes public awareness of refugee issues and co-ordinates humanitarian aid to some refugee populations. Provides the latest statistics on refugees and displaced persons. Its headquarters are in Geneva.

INDEX

ACKNOWLEDGEMENTS

The publisher is grateful for permission to reproduce the following material.

While every care has been taken to trace and acknowledge copyright, the publisher tenders its apology for any accidental infringement or where copyright has proved untraceable. The publisher would be pleased to come to a suitable arrangement in any such case with the rightful owner.

Overview

Refugees around the world, © Refugee Council, *Persons of concern*, © UNHCR, *Total asylum applications in Europe*, © ECRE, *Why do people become refugees?*, © CAFOD, *Frequently asked questions*, © Refugee Council, *Who are refugees?*, © Refugee Action, *Asylum in the UK*, © Crown Copyright is reproduced with the permission of the Controller of Her Majesty's Stationery Office, *Asylum myths*, © Oxfam, *Asylum applications in 25 European countries in 2000*, © ECRE.

Chapter One: Refugees and Asylum Seekers

Young refugees in Britain, © Children of the Storm, *Plight of the lone child refugees*, © Guardian Newspapers Limited 2001, *Young refugees*, © National Youth Agency (NYA), *Asylum-seekers*, © Save the Children, *Running for cover*, © Amnesty International, *The world of children at a glance*, © 2001 United Nations High Commission for Refugees (UNHCR), *Back to school*, © National Youth Agency (NYA), *Absent friends*, © Guardian Newspapers Limited 2002, *Cold comfort*, © Save the Children, *Refugees in Europe: the real story*, ©

Amnesty International, *The global fallout*, © 2001 United Nations High Commission for Refugees (UNHCR), *550 illegal immigrants try to storm Channel tunnel*, © Telegraph Group Limited, London 2001, *Vulnerable given a cold welcome to Britain*, © Guardian Newspapers Limited 2001, *Women refugees*, © Asylum Aid, *Racism and human rights*, © 2002, Human Rights Watch, *Top ten applicant nationalities*, © Crown Copyright is reproduced with the permission of the Controller of Her Majesty's Stationery Office, *Most asylum seekers are smuggled into Britain*, © Telegraph Group Limited, London 2001, *Asylum seekers can be detained, judges rule*, © Guardian Newspapers Limited 2001, *Asylum applications by age and gender*, © Crown Copyright is reproduced with the permission of the Controller of Her Majesty's Stationery Office, *Asylum seekers and work*, © The Industrial Society, *Asylum seekers and health*, © British Medical Association (BMA), *Protecting refugees*, © 2001 United Nations High Commission for Refugees (UNHCR), *British citizenship*, © Crown Copyright is reproduced with the permission of the Controller of Her Majesty's Stationery Office.

Photographs and illustrations:

Pages 3, 9, 37: Fiona Katauskas; pages 4, 15, 29: Pumpkin House; pages 6, 16, 20, 30, 35: Simon Kneebone; pages 13, 23, 27: Bev Aisbett.

Craig Donnellan
Cambridge
April, 2002